# "The 44 Most Closely Guarded Property Secrets"

# "The 44 Most Closely Guarded Property Secrets"

Mark Homer & Rob Moore

www.progressiveproperty.co.uk

Order this book online at www.progressiveproperty.co.uk/book-buy-now.asp

or at www.trafford.com/07-1796

Or email orders@trafford.com


Other books by Rob Moore and Mark Homer can be ordered at

www.progressiveproperty.co.uk/book2-buy-now.asp


Cover design by Nick Hillson

Photography by Nick Hillson


Most Trafford titles are also available at major online book retailers

Note for Librarians: A cataloguing record for this book is available from Library and

Archives Canada at www.collections Canada.ca/amicus/index-e.html


Printed in Peterborough, Cambridgeshire, UK


ISBN: 978-1-4251-4302-2


www.progressiveproperty.co.uk

Suites 4, 5 & 6

Queen Street Chambers

Peterborough

PE1 1PA

0845 1309505

ask@progressiveproperty.co.uk

Skype: rob.progressive

For everyone who wants to be somebody and those who know who they are.

# If it wasn't for you

**Rob** would like to thank Mark. Without him I would not have an eighth of the knowledge I have about property now. His eye for detail is inspiring [because he can do the stuff I don't like to do]. I am lucky to have such a good friend as a business partner. We built this. And we won, wasn't it sweet Mark?!

Mum for being the only person that ever hears me moan, Dad for being Dad [nuts] and actually reading this when I thought he never would [well half of it]. Arthur for the laugh, support and belief. Neil, Adam, Laura and Viv. Catherine who likes the fluff and William who simply demanded the details. Christopher and Catherine for your superb attention to detail – thanks for the extra 50 hours work guys! Everyone who is here and reading now, you are the 5%. All of you who turned your back on us when you knew we were right [you know who you are]. Thank you.

Rob Moore

robmoore@progressiveproperty.co.uk

# And if it wasn't for you

**Mark** would like to thank Mum & William. You have been a massive help in my life, in our business and in my investments. I would never have developed the Property buying skills that I have without your help. Thank You.

I would also like to thank some of the people who have helped to teach me how to buy cheap houses [whether they wanted to or not!]. Sometimes your opponents can help to make you very strong; you know who you are. Thanks.

I would also like to thank Nick Hillson, Adam Sargeson, Matt Bullock, Vanish Patel, Chris Elley [when no-one else would] Arthur Dawes, Andy Shaw - you guys have all been there for us and helped carve Progressive into what it is today.

Rob is the best business partner I could have, period. Clever, ferociously hard working, very focused, hugely competent and completely trustworthy. I thank you for all the support you have given me and for being my business partner, the future looks like an unbelievable place.

Mark Homer

markhomer@progressiveproperty.co.uk

# Contents

# Section 1: Introduction

# Section 2: The Fundamentals of Property

# Section 3: The Psychology of Successful Investors

# Section 4: The Secrets to Profit in Property: Beat the best - Retire Rich & Happy

# Section 5: What Are You Going to Do Now?

# What others have said about "The 44 Secrets..."

"As a direct result of one of the many secrets in the book, I purchased a property in Brighton for 12% BMV & have made £27,000 in 3 months, all whilst having a baby daughter! Rob & Mark actually do what they teach rather than the so called 'Guru's who talk the talk but still work in Sainsbury's at the weekend. If you have any interest whatsoever in setting yourself financially free you have to read this book now."

Neil Asher, MD New Insights: www.life-coach-training.co.uk
E-mail: neil@life-coach-training.co.uk

"Mark & Rob made me £21,000 in my first deal, saved me £1,350 in stamp duty, found and completed on the property with an instant tenant after just 76 days and I did not have to do anything except sign papers."

Richard Bellars, Inner Action Coaching: www.inneraction.co.uk
E-mail: richard@inneraction.co.uk

"What a well-written and inspiring book. I was quickly able to apply some of the techniques I learned from it to acquire an investment property which will generate profits for many years to come. I now look forward to mirroring the success of Rob and Mark, and having a substantial portfolio of income-generating properties in the not too distant future"

Richard Clifford: richard.clifford@gmail.com

"One of, if not the best investment I've ever made! This information is not only timely and informative, but it actually works. I've learnt more from your book than all of the courses I've attended. I wish I'd have read this before spending £7,000 on property courses! I'd be a few steps closer to my dream of becoming financially free! I'm Looking forward to reading the next one, and making a killing off the 'Property Crash'! Keep up the good work"

Dan Atkins: www.atkinsinvestment.co.uk

"I just couldn't put it down. I read the whole book cover to cover in less than 5 hours. I now realise you can make money in a boom or a crash and not to listen to anything the papers say! This book makes me want to go out and get cash and invest NOW. For very little money you can build a portfolio worth millions of pounds.

Adam Sargeson: adam_sargeson@jpress.co.uk

"Gents, I have just finished the above book and I must congratulate you. My synopsis would be "An holistic approach to Property investment for long term financial security"
I had a strong sense of Andy Shaw meets Anthony Robbins, which is not a bad combination for success. I personally followed your model and bought 3 local properties which have proved to be excellent buys. "

Gary Moore

# Section 1: Introduction

Rob Moore & Mark Homer

Rob Moore & Mark Homer

Firstly an apology [of sorts]. This book has been written by the two people you see named on the front cover. That's us: hi! Rob is the tall one with the crazy shirt and slightly red beard. Mark has hair on his head and not on his face; it's a pleasure to meet you.

Throughout the course of talking to you, we flick between I and we. This must surely break all literary rules. We did try an edit in the first person, but it just didn't work. We felt that this is the best way to get across the voices of both of us, and to give you alternative perspectives. Some rules are just there to be broken.

This book is the combined knowledge of Rob and Mark, whose skills lie in different areas. If it were not for Rob this book would never have been written, and if it were not for Mark a great deal of this Property knowledge would still be somewhere in the ether; rendering it useless.

At any one point in this book you could be speaking to me [or me], or both of us. Know that we work very closely together and rely on each other to power forward in our business and personal lives. We would not be where we are today [which is a place of contentment and enjoyment] without each other's help, support and specific areas of focus.

Most people would tell you not to go into business with a friend. Don't. But if you can go into business with someone you trust and who becomes a great friend, then you are fortunate. We are fortunate – not lucky – and we hope that this helps bring a

Rob Moore & Mark Homer

wide range of useful tools for your investment success and future financial independence.

And shed loads of money [if that is ok with you]. More about that later.

And more about us a little bit later. If you do want to read more about us you can go straight to the back. But as we said, that is not the purpose of this book.

**Special upfront offer**

If you missed, have not read or did not receive our free bonuses worth £247 that came along with buying this book then please feel free now to log on to this page:

www.progressiveproperty.co.uk/free-offer-now.asp

# What You can expect from this book

This book has been designed to be *the* most comprehensive guide to making profit from investment Property ever written, that is accessible to most people.

A big claim perhaps?

We are by no means professing to be the biggest pair of 'Guru's' in the Property universe. We are both relatively young [which is why you can do it too] and still have much work to do. We have much to learn and hundreds more properties to buy for ourselves, and our close community of investors.

We have, however, read most of the Property books out there. Some are good, some are average; most have at least some useful stuff in them. Some are quite complicated and others just a taster, leaving you needing more. What we aim to achieve here is a mix of most of those that focus on how you can actually apply the money making strategies into your own life. More than just the concepts; the specifics.

What we are trying to say is that we wanted to write a book for you. If a pair of cheeky 20 something year olds can do it; then so can you!

We could have beefed this up too, you know. 500 pages at £25 or put it in a manual with more gaps and charged £197 for it [and it would still be worth every penny]. But we wanted this to

Rob Moore & Mark Homer

be precise, to the point and something you can carry around with you.

If, after reading this book, you feel that we have not lived up to this, or that there has been no realisable value in what we have written, we will give you your money back, no questions asked.

Actually we probably will ask why, because your opinion matters to us, but we'll still stand by our guarantee.

We feel that we have seen so much [and the road is never ending] that if you are just starting out, or even if you have been investing for years, you **need** to know this information if you want to make money from Property.

It's all too easy to think we are making money when in fact we're losing it hand over fist. If we can help you avoid the mistakes most investors make, then this book has been worth the years, the money, the fun, the pain, the working all night every night for 6 months and the sweat we have put into it.

Why would we offer a money back guarantee on a book? Surely that is ridiculous and unnecessary. Some businessmen might go so far as to call us idiots. Hey ho.

That is a risk we are willing to take to prove to you, before you start, that we feel that there is so much truth out there that you are not being told by most people or companies.

We reckon that 1% of you who read this will want your money back. Now we know that it won't be you, but it will be someone. They are the ones who are too tight to take the information and see more benefit in getting the cash back, the ones who know that they can't be bothered to do anything about it and so see value in getting some beer money back, or the ones who think we are talking utter toilet.

And fair enough to all three.

If you do decide to return it please send it back to Progressive Property where we will refund your investment. All of our details are at the back of the book.

We are confident enough in what we have learned and experienced [mostly through attrition, ambition, inadvertence, fortune and some misfortune], that we really believe that 99% of you will not want your investment back. The fact is that you have put your hand in your pocket, even if it is only a small investment, and that says a lot. Thank You! We believe you will want to use this book long into the future for reference to build your portfolio. And you should. You might even enjoy it too.

Use it as a manual, use it as a guide, use it as a checklist of do's and don'ts, use it to motivate and inspire you to take action. Use it as a warning as to what and who to watch out for, use it as a beer mat or use it to reach the Jaffa cakes on the top shelf of the cupboard.

Rob Moore & Mark Homer

Just make sure you use it.

And if at the end of the book you still think to yourself:
'I don't have the time'

'I'm not interested in doing it myself'

Then we will offer you a way that you can have it all without
putting any of your own time or effort in. We will offer you an
**even easier** way to make money in Property.

Does that sound fair enough?

But you must read all the way to the end of the book to qualify
for this, and you will be very glad that you did!

## What's new?

For a couple of years now we have been commenting in our
office on the lack of Property books that educate. Books that
you can read and then go out into the real world and apply
what you have just read.

I [Rob] recently read a well presented book on affiliate
marketing which talked at great lengths on how the author had
made millions of dollars on the internet. However at the end of
the book I didn't feel like I knew any different, other than the
fact that he had done it. I did not feel that I could actually go

and do it for myself – there were no real strategies I could take and apply in the 'Real World.'

When there has been an area where we have needed to learn, we have rarely been able to find a book written to speed our education.

If you want to learn about Google Adwords or fishing or cross-stitch, there are thousands of books out there. If you want to learn about Property, you have to actually do it. You can't [as of writing] do a GCSE or A-Level in Buy to Let investing and you can't take it at University.

We hope to change this now.

Even if there were a Property option at University we daresay that we may not have studied too hard on anything that did not involve a public house or a single, attractive female. For us it has all happened just as it was supposed to.

We do believe that there should be more practical education in the areas of investment and securing your financial future [not get rich quick]; hence writing this book. We shall not go into detail here, as this book is for people who want to make serious and long lasting profits in Property.

However, books such as 'Think and Grow Rich', 'Rich Dad, Poor Dad' and 'The Richest Man in Babylon' certainly helped ingrain the financial principles in us that we believe are essential tools to have in any successful wealth arsenal.

You can get them directly from our website, along with many other great books that have inspired us:

www.progressiveproperty.co.uk/readinglist.asp

We hope that this book fills this educational void for you that we felt there is [was!] in Property education. We also hope that you will be able to take what you've read here and go out straight away and make it happen for you. Believe us; you really can if you choose to. Commit to it now.

This book will reveal all: the good, the bad and the downright disgusting about Property investment. You absolutely positively must read this before you even think about investing. Don't part with your cash until you have finished whatever you do. Chain yourself to the sofa and don't get up until you're done!

If we had read and learned the 'secrets' within this book before investing, we would have saved ourselves many mistakes. We would have saved a hell of a lot of money too. However all mistakes are part of our journey. You can benefit now from these and learn from our mistakes, in the hope that you can get it right from the start and make Property investment work for you [even quicker than we did].

And save a wad of cash in the meantime.

Rob Moore & Mark Homer

# What You won't get from this book

Tripe.

A common phrase used in our office to describe all that is cloak and dagger, smoke and mirror, embellishment, porkie pie and utter rubbish.

Yes we'll try to get you excited about the things that are exciting now, and we hope that you do. If we are not enjoying ourselves then what is the point of it all?

What we are interested in talking about is what actually works in *reality*. What we have learned applied and got real results from that we have measured. What we know to be the truth based on our own personal experience. We'll touch on everything else that doesn't work, and sometimes we may get on our high horse a little, please humour us and let us get it all out, it makes us feel better!

Just know that proof and speculation are very different 'investment' propositions.

Our disclaimer:
We have taken care to make the figures and specifics in this book as accurate and relevant as possible at the time of writing; and of course we hope you understand that these can change dependent on market and economic forces.

Rob Moore & Mark Homer

The content, projections, figures and indications contained in this book are based on opinion and cannot be relied upon when making investment decisions. As with any investment, Property values can fall as well as rise.

The Authors offer this information as a guide only and it cannot be considered as financial advice in any way. Please refer to your independent financial advisor who is qualified to give you complete advice based on your circumstances.

The authors Rob Moore and Mark Homer are not qualified to give mortgage, legal or financial advice. Please seek legal and financial advice from a qualified advisor before making commitments. Neither its authors nor 'Progressive Property Ltd' accept liability for decisions made based on the content of this book.

Of course that was necessary to get out of the way and it is something that you know already. This book is a guide and you have ultimate *choice*.

If you are looking for MLM [Multi Level Marketing], get rich quick, zero to a million in 15 minutes, 'exciting opportunity' [that will be a healthcare ponzi you can be sure], home based biz, £500 per month without having to work [read from the back of a car or on a lamppost], or anything that promises the earth and delivers earth, then you are not reading the right book.

Stop now.

Honestly. We don't want to waste your time. We know that it is really alluring and shiny, but everything comes at a cost in life. Now we know that we are both only kids and many investors are old enough to be our grandfathers, so we still have plenty to learn in life, but one thing that really is true is that the world does not owe us a living. [And the fact that we are still both well under 30 should really inspire you right now. We did it. You can do it. It's that simple.]

There is no easy shortcut to wealth that does not involve silver cutlery or a golden ticket, so don't even bother looking for it. In fact be so cynical about all of the above 'opportunities' and demand absolute proof that they work, because that is exactly the kind of attitude we need to become serious and successful Property investors who have a chance of making something of our lives.

And some money. Oh yeah.

Take it all as education. I [Rob] was keenly involved in an MLM business a few years back with total [yet ignorant] belief that it was going to set me 'financially free.' Mark thought it was ridiculous [not the words he used!] and despite terrible pressure [not from me], refused to have any active involvement.

I worked so hard and was totally committed to my future and was convinced that everyone who joined would become loaded without having to do anything, because that is what they made us believe.

As it often seems to turn out, many of these companies are not diligent; they have no knowledge of systems or duplication, they give no guidance, support or back up and rarely pay commissions. They whip everyone into a frenzy to sign up but often don't deliver on their promises [not all of them; this is just our personal experience]. All the hard work and friends and family that I had got involved were left high and dry of nearly £300 [most of which I paid].

This is commonplace in this market and Mark was right and that is why I love working with him. He is right most of the time, especially when it comes to Property. I do manage to get him occasionally though, and I don't let him forget it.

## About Rob & Mark

At the end of this book, there are a few pages that tell you about us. Because this book is for you, we thought that the back is the best place for them. What we do think is relevant to you now, is how we got to where we are and how you can do the same. A small introduction:

*Mark* bought his first Property in 2004:

I started buying small houses because I realised that the smaller properties [under £125,000] in our area were growing quicker when compared to anything over £150,000. I saw it as a reduced risk to chop my money into smaller properties rather than buying expensive ones, and knew that most people want to rent cheaper houses rather than 5 Bed Mansions with swimming pools and cinema rooms [which I couldn't afford anyway].

Having spent ages researching [I have a bit of a habit of over-analysing] I found **one street** in Peterborough that I felt was massively undervalued compared to other streets in the same area of the same type.

I must have bought most of this street and was only spending about £3,000 on a full redecoration. I was buying the properties at around £75,000. I was getting them cheap anyway because I was negotiating good discounts, and I was **convinced** that they were worth up to £100,000.

I wanted to get all of my money back out of the properties so that I could keep buying more on the same street without any extra cash. I put them all on the market at the same time for what I thought they were really worth. I then got a surveyor round to value them and gave him the comparables of my other houses that I had recently put on the market. I had a couple that were not valued as high as I wanted so once I got a surveyor that valued one of my properties at the price I wanted, I got him to value all of the others. He valued them all at the price I believed they were worth.

Rob Moore & Mark Homer

As a result I was able to remortgage these properties almost instantly after revaluation and get all of my money back [deposit, all fees and refurb costs] and extra cash on top, because of the discount I had got and the value I had added by doing some small refurbishment work.

I kept going until I had pushed the value of the whole street so high that I could not get the properties as cheap anymore. But that was fine because I owned a load of them and they were all free!

And sure enough, as I had predicted, the market grew and the properties continued to go up. In 2 years the properties I bought have gone up over 50%.

I knew I now had a system that I could just replicate all over Peterborough. All I had to do was locate the areas that were undervalued with good rents and buy as many as I could using the same strategy.

I love it. It has helped me build a substantial portfolio and we are using the same system to help our investors do the same.

**Rob** started Property investment in 2005 having thought about it for 4 years without taking any action:

Within 3 months of learning this strategy I had already remortgaged my house that I had bought 3 years before. My house had gone up from £125,000 to £170,000 in that time.

The funny thing is that I had made £45,000 in 3 years doing nothing at all, from that one Property.

I was an 'accidental investor' like so many people who own their own house are. I didn't even know that I was literally sitting on a Goldmine, and that one house would help me build an asset base worth many millions.

As an Artist, in that same 3 years, I had struggled working 14 hours or more every day just to earn the same amount of money.

I didn't even buy it at discount; I paid full asking price for it. My Dad helped me raise the deposit. My diligence and market research went as far as: it's next door to Mum and Dad, I want it!

When I remortgaged my repayments went down from £750 per month to £550 per month. **And** I released £26,000 cash. This was because I had not got the best rate at that time, and because I was on a capital repayment mortgage.

With that remortgage I paid off all of my credit cards and loans [which saved me around £1500 per month] and with what was left I bought another 7 properties, with Mark, in the space of 4 months. I built a portfolio that was worth well over £1million [which keeps going up] before that year was even over. Since that time we have not stopped buying Property together and we never will.

Rob Moore & Mark Homer

Why would we? You may not either. Stop, that is.

I literally went from being nearly £30,000 in debt to having a portfolio that could fund the rest of my life, all in less than 6 months. I am certainly nothing 'special', I was no expert at the time, and Mark had most of the knowledge back then. The one thing I am proud of is that I was **decisive**. I found the strategy that worked and I took immediate action. I have never looked back.

Our portfolio has grown significantly since then and we have built Progressive, helping other people do the same. And I love it.

## Enough sizzle, where's my steak?

So that is more than enough about the two of us. Hopefully that has helped you feel excited about what you are about to learn now.

If you do not feel excited by now then you should be. What you are about to read, if applied and persevered with, will absolutely guarantee your future financial success, security and happiness.

It is that simple.

Bring it on? You want it? Well here we go...

One more thing: a huge thank you for buying our book, it really means a lot to us.

Rob Moore & Mark Homer

# Section 2: The Fundamentals of Property

Rob Moore & Mark Homer

In this section, we aim to run over with you the fundamental basics you need to get you going buying Property. Some of this might seem quite obvious to you, which is just fine, because it is very important. It won't be a bad thing to go over it again and embed it in your subconscious now.

However there are many things that we regard as basic that many investors either ignore or do not understand, and so we believe that this will be of benefit to you. More of the tricks and secrets come in section 4. You will need the knowledge in this section before moving on through.

If you know most [or all] of this then you are ahead of the game and should be excited now about what you will achieve: section 4 will build on your knowledge. If all of this is new, then be excited that you have just saved yourself years of mistakes that we would have loved to avoid.

Enjoy and know that just by reading it is all starting to happen...

Rob Moore & Mark Homer

# Why invest?

Why not just spend our money on cars, conservatories, holidays and feed our eBay and online gambling addictions and be done with it? After all, we only live once and we can't take it with us, right?

Fair enough. Go and join the lottery winners who won it all, spent it all, and ended up in more debt 3 years down the line [there was one chap who lived just a few miles from us who did exactly that]. Oh, and don't forget your one in 3 squillion chance of success [or 14,000,000:1 actual figure – thanks Chris!] that relies on luck.

What we are talking about here is financial independence. It's about building an asset base steadily and properly; investing your time and money at the start so that you can reap the rewards in the future.

Set up once and earn forever.

You are planting your money tree to produce your golden apples year after year *for the rest of your life*. If you cut the tree down before it matures [as most people do] then it will never produce your golden fruit. Let's pull out all the clichés: you wouldn't slay the golden goose, who lays the golden eggs, would you?

It's all about delaying some of that instant gratification and thinking mid - long term, because it will not be long before you can start picking those apples, and collecting those golden eggs, as long as your tree and goose are ready.

**Financial independence**: it has been said that you cannot work or save your way to financial independence, which is defined as the 'length of time that you can comfortably live without the need to work or exchange time for money.'

Indeed many of us have got into the trap of working more and more, yet not achieving the happiness or lifestyle that we really want, haven't we?

At Progressive it is our true purpose to help you to financial independence. This is inherent in our mission and another reason for writing this book. We know of other investors and Property educators who charge £3,000 and more on courses, and they will not tell you any more [or even as much] as what is in these 370 odd pages.

Don't get us wrong, we do have personal reasons for teaching you this. We want testimonials. We want success stories. We want to be part of your success and we would love to use your story to help us promote what we already know you can do. You can also be part of our success and help us grow.

We believe that it is the right of everyone to be in a position of financial independence, that there is more than enough money in the world for us all to be millionaires [if we really want it], and that there is a simple system that we can follow in order to achieve the lifestyle we desire. Yet another reason for the conception of this book.

Without investing capital [money] and making our money work for us, we will never be in a position to do the things in life that we really want to do. A savings account is no longer enough, due to low interest and high inflation. As soon as we start to live from savings they diminish, and money from earnings will only come for as long as we are working.

If you hang like an Orang-utan from the branches of your golden apple tree before it has grown to bear fruit; they will snap.

Knowing that we do have a *choice*, what choice is it for you now?

Working [exchanging time for money] will never make us financially independent. As soon as we lose our ability to work [through burn out, illness, injury, loss of motivation, family commitments, lack of desire, laziness] we no longer have income. None of us want that do we?

One thing that hit us was the relationship between money and stress. We looked at all the people we knew: our parents, friends, mentors, business associates and so on. We realised that those who were stressed were the ones who were working for their money. We've all been there, haven't we?

Rob Moore & Mark Homer

And the more they worked for their money, the more stressed they became. Yes, this might be a shift in thinking and not 'traditional', but when people have to work for money they end up getting stressed [or worse] almost every time.

So we decided to shift our thinking. Remember, everything starts with ourselves. What if we could earn money without working? What if we could earn money without doing something we hate, and without the stress? You can imagine what people thought about that. Of course, stubborn as we are, we ignored them. We shall deal with 'pub talk' later.

Property is one of the best vehicles that allows you to earn money without working. Our lives have changed dramatically since investing in Property, and we have grown to have a burning passion for Property investment [an added bonus!].

Oh, and did you know that over 40% of the Times 100 Rich List have earned fortunes through Property investment?

Of all the investment vehicles we have looked at [and we have looked at many] Property is the best, in our opinion, from the following viewpoints:

The leverage that you can attain through Property is like no other investment vehicle available. We explain leverage in more detail later on. You can leverage your money 10 times over with just a standard 90% mortgage, and that is without factoring in any growth on your portfolio.

Stocks and shares do not enable the average investor to leverage their money; nor does a savings account. You earn only on your money invested, not the bank's money [all will be explained later].

"All this talk of Property, shares and investment, why not just keep your money in the bank earning 5% per year and be done with it? Surely the bank is the safest way to save your money?"

This question comes up regularly. Or "why not keep your red lobsters [£50 notes apparently] under the mattress with the sawn-off shotgun," no one will get their hands on it then!

OK, let's look at this. We like talking about this because most people don't realise how little banks actually incentivise [not a word? It's one we like to use] you to save with them.

With inflation currently somewhere near 3% [the RPI is over 4% at the time of writing] the value of your money is going down at 3% per year. We actually believe that the true rate of inflation is much higher, and the government may perhaps be trying to cover it up, but this is not a conspiracy theory book! One thing we don't know is that the cost of food, petrol, many commodities, and general living, are very much on the rise. Immediately cash is worth much less every year, so at least 3% of your 5% interest has just been eaten. Damn it!

Then there is the increase in the cost of living. Currently this is going up at a greater rate than salary rises, so more money is lost to the expense of general living. Annoying.

Then there is tax. Oh tax. Bloody tax. The government charge you tax on interest gained at your tax rate of up to 40%, so that eats another 1-2%, leaving you with less money than you had last year.

It's a complete joke [but it's not funny].

So if anyone tries to tell you that leaving your money in the bank will make you a nice tasty 5% per year, then I'm afraid that they are wrong [or on narcotics]. You are actually losing money at the rate of over 1% per year [on a good day].

Leave your cash under your mattress and you are losing around 5% per year at the moment [and going insane with paranoia].

Most people don't understand this. Just knowing how to work out the true costs of an investment will set your expectations at the right level from the start, enabling you to make some good returns without getting burned.

That's inflation. Interestingly, as inflation goes up, and the value of money goes down, the values of Property continue to rise. Surely then it makes sense to leave the majority of your money there in your portfolio?

Does this make sense?

But won't the Government look after me?  Yeah right. Let's get real here, things are not as they used to be. I [Rob] learned this about 3 years before writing this book and realised then that the only person who would look after my future was me. Bear this in mind: *no one is going to look after your future but you*.

We don't need to talk too much about pensions in this book as we all seem to agree that pension stability and security are relics of the past. Gone is the industrial age where you worked for the same company for 25 years and the state pension took care of the rest.

The government increase taxes year on year to repay their national debt. Many of our greatest assets have been sold off [British Gas, BA, BT, Jag, Aston Martin] and the last point of financial return for our government is the tax-paying public.

That's you and us.

When you actually work it out some of us pay upwards of 70% of our money in taxes. We pay tax on what we earn, on what we buy, on what we sell, on services we provide and receive. We pay tax on places we go and methods in which we travel.

Think of a car: we pay tax on our income to raise the money for it. We pay tax to the bank for saving it. We pay tax to buy it. We pay tax to insure it. We pay tax to tax it. We pay tax to put fuel in it. We pay tax to fix it. The bigger car we get the more tax we pay. We pay tax to drive it to some cities. We pay tax when we drive it too fast. We pay tax to park it. We pay tax to park it 5 minutes longer than we said we would park it.

You get the picture. End of rant.

## Summary

The only way to achieve financial independence is to invest. The government will not look after you. Savings are not enough. Stashing cash will make you paranoid. You control your future; no one else will take care of it for you.

# The Law of compounding

Money attracts Money.

It is said that like attracts like, and money is no different. Einstein called the Law of compounding the 8th wonder of the world. He believed it was a Law, and that is what we would like us to discuss here, if that's ok with you.

A great analogy is one of a bet on a golf course: betting £1 per hole and doubling your bet on each hole seems like a fairly innocuous challenge. However that £1 bet compounded over each hole turns into £256 in 9 holes.

Quite a compounded effect isn't it? Well that's nothing. After hole 15 that amount has compounded to £16,384. Look at how much more money is being attracted now. Once we get to hole 18 the compounded effect is £131,072.

It is this straightforward: the more money you invest, the greater the returns you will get. And the beauty of it is that it all started from £1, but it was not spent; the returns were re-invested [and compounded].

There is also a classic riddle [we've played with the figures to make them even more interesting] where a child is offered 2 options for an increasingly weekly pocket money allowance:

Option 1: £20 per week for 20 weeks

Option 2: £0.01 per week for 20 weeks doubled [compounded] every week

Now what child in their right mind [or even some of us for that matter!] wouldn't take the £20 per week?

Here are the results:

Option 1:

At week 5: £100

Weeks 5-10: £100

Weeks 10-15: £100

Weeks 15- 20: £100

Total: £400

Option 2:

At week 5: £0.32

Weeks 5-10: £10.24

Weeks 10-15: £327.68

Weeks 15- 20: £10,485.76

Total: £20,872.96

Pretty powerful, isn't it?! And a good lesson in the value of thinking long term too, don't you think?!

Even more relevant for you when thinking about Property and the money you invest is 'The Rule of 72.' This law, or formula, demonstrates the Law of compounding very well. We use it here for illustrational purposes and to show the impact of the Law of compounding, and of course you could use this in many of your future investments.

To estimate the amount of time required to double an original investment, divide the most convenient "rule-quantity" [72] by the expected growth rate, expressed as a percentage.

For instance, if you were to invest £1000 with compounding interest at a rate of 9% per annum, the rule of 72 gives 72/9 = 8 years required for the investment to be worth £2000; an exact calculation gives 8.0432 years.

We like playing with this. If we add some relevant Property figures to this equation it starts to get very interesting:

You buy a £100,000 Property for £85,000. This is something that you can easily do using the principles in this book.

To cut to the chase, and keep it simple, a deal like this will probably cost you about £3,000 to £5,000. We'll explain later how we get to that figure, it's not important for this example.

We know that Property grows at an average of 11.74% per year [source: Nationwide house price statistics]. You can put some figures in based on your expectation of growth or your attitude to risk. We can use the rule of 72 and put our figures in like this:

Rob Moore & Mark Homer

5% growth: 72/5 = 14.4 years to turn £5,000 into £10,000
8% growth: 72/8 = 9 years to turn £5,000 into £10,000
11.74% growth = 72/11.74 = 6 years 48 days to turn £5,000
into £10,000

Once you start adding leverage to this, you'll see just how powerful this can become very quickly indeed. More about that later.

It doesn't matter where you are in your current position. If you have very little money [or quite a lot of debt] you can still apply this Law. As long as you obey the other concepts in this book ['Laws'] then you will turn not much into a lot in a very short space of time.

As we shall discuss frequently as we go, always be looking at how you can leverage what you have and compound it to make very large sums of money. If you have equity in your home, or know someone who does, then you should be particularly excited to read on now.

Don't we always hear people pointing out how the rich get richer and the poor get poorer? Well this is generally the case as they are attracting more of what they already have; be that wealth and abundance or bills and more bills a 'lack' mentality. And they understand the principles that we have shown you in this section:

"I have a problem with too much money. I can't reinvest it fast enough, and because I reinvest it, more money comes in. Yes, the rich do get richer." Robert Kiyosaki

Look at your Property wealth strategy [coming up in a few minutes] and make sure you invest and re-invest. Take money for expenditure and by all means enjoy it, but only within your percentages, and the strategy that you have set for yourself.

We want to help you to think mid - long term here. This will be mentioned many times in the book. When you plant a seed you can't come back the next day and expect it to be a huge fruit bearing apple tree that your kids can climb. You have to water it, give it sunlight and rich nutrients in the soil. You have to look after it and be patient with it. When you are, it will bear fruit for you year after year after year.

The 'Law' of compounding works just this way. And remember, it works just as effectively in reverse with debt. Treat it with total respect and you can grow your Property portfolio to look after you and your family for generations to come, without you having to work again.

## Summary

Money attracts money. Invest and re-invest and watch your money multiply like gremlins [just add water]. Understand and apply the Law of compounding and build a solid foundation that you can live from for the rest of your life.

# Why Property & not the lottery?

Now we are starting to talk about Property and the benefits over saving and other investment vehicles. Very nice indeed; we love talking about Property.

You know, so many people tell us that they have been thinking about investing in Property for years and years, but have never done anything about it [for whatever reason]. Here are just a few we've heard first hand:

"I haven't got any money. If [when] I had more money I could invest."

"Other people don't want me to. My Mum/Dad/mates think I'm insane to even think about it."

"I don't have the time. I'm just too busy."

"I don't know enough people. I don't know any investors."

"I'm not educated enough. I didn't go to a good school: what do I know about money and Property?"

"The market is going to crash. I have been saying it for the last 10 years, d'ya know wha' I mean?"

So what makes Property so good that we keep on shouting about it? And what do we know about other vehicles of investment to compare it to?

There are many fundamental reasons why we believe that Property is the best investment vehicle for long term wealth. Here they are all nicely broken down for you:

**The Basics**: first and foremost Property [shelter] is a basic human requirement. It is just below the need for air and food, and on a par with the need to interact with other human beings. It is way above the need for money, cars, designer clothes, handbags and matching shoes, the latest golf clubs and cosmetic skincare products [or at least it should be, come on!]

As long as we're alive we'll need housing. We will always need shelter from the cold and the rain and the snow and the wind.

So what? What does that mean in investment terms for you? It means consistent and perpetual demand. Add to that the fact that we are an island here in the UK, and the population is growing year on year; what do you think is going to happen to that demand? You guessed it. We shall talk about demand later. Even if we do get to inhabit Mars or live in space, we will still need shelter [probably lots of metal and air conditioning].

**Touch it, Feel it**: Property is tangible. It is real. You can see it, touch it, visit it, walk through it, and as a result control it much more than many other investments.

With shares in companies you do not have that added security.

Look at the dotcom crash and the fall of the Nasdaq. Many of those so called multi-million dollar companies were so intangible that their true values were highly volatile and questionable. Many of them were ultimately proven to be speculative and worth very little.

**The Control Freak in You and Me**: anything you can see and you're close to, you have a certain amount of control over. If your dog is on a lead you can guide him, pull him away from the kids that walk by, and scoop up the mess he leaves behind. Other dogs can even follow his trail and sniff exactly the path he has been down.

Take a speculative company based in someone's bedroom in Taiwan; how can you control that? How can you feel comfortable about your money being in companies you will never ever see?

The answer is that you can't. As will become very apparent, anything that can't be reasonably controlled will not provide you with the kind of investment you want [if you are looking for mid - long term financial independence and security that is]. And perhaps you want a chance of making some money with a little bit of freedom and happiness to boot?!

**Property vs. Shares**: pound for pound, stocks and Property perform quite closely. Some will tell you that Property will outperform shares every time and others will tell you vice versa.

In our experience it is far easier to utilise *leverage* in Property. We have met many people who have told us that you can make 6% per month on shares by renting them out; all you have to do is turn your computer on once a month!

Funnily enough they sell these educational packs with huge 'thud factors' at big seminars and charge thousands of pounds for them. They would tell you that now wouldn't they?

Out of all the people that we have met who have bought these, or been exposed to them, we have never actually met anybody that has made them work or given us evidence. Even these 'Gurus' don't seem to be doing it themselves, which makes us wonder...

You cannot go to a bank and ask for a loan for £100,000 to go and put on the stock market, on trap 6 or all on black. Interesting, isn't it, that companies are queuing up to loan the average Joe or Jo money against a house, but no one will touch anyone who is not Warren Buffet [with a bargepole] to lend money to invest in shares.

To the average or good investor Property offers the best solutions. I know that there are people who really are experts in the stock market who are making cash and using other people's money to make that cash. But these guys have been doing it for 30 years. They are proven experts.

**History**: history tells us that Property is one of the most sound and powerful investment vehicles available.

Since records began in the 1950's Property has performed remarkably well, doubling in value every 7-10 years as an average. You can get the sources of all of the following statistics on our site, where we link to all of the relevant and reputable sources:

www.progressiveproperty.co.uk/latestpropertynews.asp

Using history as an effective gauge; it tells us that Property is, has been and will continue to be a superb investment.

Remember that we said that we're always looking for evidence when gathering data for our investments? Well the last 55 years is a great place to start.

History is not a guarantee of what is to come, but it is a good indicator of what is likely to happen over a long period of time. This is what we, as investors, need to know.

According to The Halifax plc: UK Property prices have risen in 36 out of the past 40 years, seeing an average annual increase of 10.3%.

**Demand for Property is currently at a very high point**: 'demand for housing is increasing over time, driven primarily by demographic trends and rising incomes,' according to the

Barker report. With the typical family unit breaking up much more frequently, with larger families, higher divorce rates, and a huge influx of migrants, demand is outweighing supply at around 120,000 homes per year.

We really could go into serious detail in this section about all of the evidence suggesting that Property will be a secure investment for your financial security and independence. However we don't want to bore the pants off you, and this brief overview can be followed up on our site should you desire the details. We would strongly suggest after reading this book that you do go and read up on Property, and make your own decisions about the risks involved:

www.progressiveproperty.co.uk

**Market movements**: in the UK we have a far greater chance of success than the vast majority of the rest of the world. We experience strong Property ownership rights and in general our Property market is very strong here in the UK. Long term demand is based on an acute shortage of properties [homes]. Figures of which can be seen here:

www.progressiveproperty.co.uk/downloads/Progressive-Market-Analysis.pdf

Times are very very interesting [and exciting for a select few] at the moment. Opportunity is massive but most people will miss it all and wonder what the hell happened. The secret to buying

Property at 30% below market value is still unknown by the majority. If you would like to learn how to massively profit, and make large amounts of cash in a Property market 'crash' right now, go to:

www.progressiveproperty.co.uk/book2-buy-now.asp

**Affordability in the market**: "aren't properties just too expensive for first time buyers at the moment?"

Well yes, house prices are going up. This is great news for those of us who are buying. Properties will always go up over the long term: history has told us that for the last 55 years, remember?

And guess what happens to rents when prices go up?! That's right, they catch up [and go up].

As a side note: between 2004 and the back end of 2007 we personally experienced very strong growth in our own portfolio. Obviously good, right? However, what miffed us was that our rents across the board had not gone up a penny.

There is always a lag between the increase in Property values and the rising of rents, and between November 2007 and March 2008 our average rents have shot up by 20%! This has been caused by the strong increase in prices, causing more people to rent than buy due to a lack of affordability.

The market has to adapt to this. As much as people [and the press] might scaremonger, it is highly unlikely that, all of a sudden, all first time buyers will all be out on the streets. There is evidence to suggest that people are living in smaller [and smaller] properties in this country, as the availability of Property decreases and prices rise. This has forced the market to adapt to provide ways in which first time buyers can afford to get on the ladder.

Markets always adapt - as they are doing in the UK, which contradicts the common misconception that this 'can't go on any longer.' Vendor paid deposits, micro flats, shared ownership and friends buying together are further examples of ways that people can still access the market despite higher prices.

Mortgages are now being offered over longer periods as a natural response to reduced affordability. The old maxim of a 25 year mortgage is now being stretched with more than a quarter of lenders offering lending for up to 40 years. Split mortgages can also be obtained where up to 5 people can share the ownership of a single Property.

The average size of homes in London and Tokyo are extremely small compared to the rest of the world, but this wasn't always the case. They have had to adapt over time for the same reasons.

For an example of market adaptation, look at the change in residential developments: we have smaller plots, where gardens and footprints are compensated by additional storeys. Many houses are now 'town houses' with 3 floors as opposed to 2.

As demand for land and Property [price per square foot] has increased, there has been a shift to living in smaller properties. This has allowed prices to continue rising whilst not pricing people out of the market. People who have already bought have benefited from these increased Property values.

And remember, we live on a very small island. Land will always be at a premium, especially when compared to countries like the US. This should keep driving the price of Property upwards, enabling investors like us to continue to gain long term returns.

Make money.

**Demand Outweighing Supply**: the shortage of homes which we now face here in the UK [great news for rental demand] has been brought about by a number of factors.

Migration into the UK has affected demand, along with an increase in people living alone. This creates a smaller average household size, as does divorce and larger family units that split.

The rate of house building in the UK is not keeping pace with demand. In 2005 193,000 new homes were built. Although this was the highest for 15 years, it is still only 3/4 of the number

Rob Moore & Mark Homer

that the government's independent report estimated would be required each year to bring house price inflation down to 1%. The current shortfall is around 120,000 new homes per year according to the 2003 Barker Report. By 2021 The Halifax predicts that the shortfall will have reached 400,000 per year.

To reiterate: the demand for Property is **far** outweighing supply, keeping prices high: all very positive evidence for future investment in Property **for the long term**.

**Growth in Buy to Let in the UK**: the UK rental market has grown significantly since the introduction of Assured Shorthold Tenancies [AST] and Buy to Let mortgages in 1996. Between 1995 and 2003 the number of people needing to rent doubled from 46,000 to over 93,000, according to the Barker report. This means more tenants for investors like you and us. This trend has continued, with demand for **the right types of rental properties**_in the **correct areas** remaining strong.

Another effect of continuing price growth has been the increased difficulties first time buyers face when buying Property. This has fuelled rental demand even more as more of the population need to rent for longer before being able to buy.

Increased levels of personal spending have also created a situation where people save less and so don't have the deposit monies available to gain a mortgage.

On average, rents in the UK have doubled every 9 to 12 years through history, and we have one of the most competitive Buy to Let mortgage markets in the world. Interest rates are relatively low and lending environments are efficient.

All great evidence and positive news for Property investment, don't you think?

More importantly, we think, is that Property gives you freedom and choice. Just as we explained the benefits of investing over spending and saving, Property is the vehicle that will allow you to live the life that you choose. Because your properties will be growing year on year without you having to work on them, you are free to do as you please, with all the money you need and more.

## Summary

Property is tangible and real. You can see and control it. It is secure and much less volatile compared to other investments. History and demand all point to a great future for Property investment and for you.

Rob Moore & Mark Homer

# Leverage

Leverage is an Art form in a scientific guise.

If you can master the Art of leverage then you will be wealthy beyond all of your expectations, plans, goals [and quite possibly dreams]. You will earn on your portfolio almost infinitely more than you would using your own money.

Leverage is becoming more and more important in our society. This has been a massive learning for us over the last 2 years, and has exponentially changed our quality of life since 2004/5.

First there was the donkey, the camel, the horse and the elephant. We're not great on history, so we can't tell you which one came first. Did prehistoric man use the mammoth to get from his Ice house to the local Ice Bar? You get the picture; we used animals to make a journey quicker and easier.

Then there was the wheel 3000 odd years B.C. Then the bicycle, then the train, then the car, then the plane, then the shuttle. Who knows what will come next, but whatever it is will make journeys even faster and easier.

In the modern day we have the internet; a huge vehicle for leveraging time. More recently businesses turn to P.A's, virtual assistants [V.A's] and outsourcing to leverage our time more cheaply than employing full time people or doing the work ourselves and dying at 65!

Rob Moore & Mark Homer

Leverage is so important if you want to achieve more with less effort. It can be a hard shift; people take real ownership of things that they have built and can get precious about handing tasks over to other people; yet think nothing about using a taxi to get to the newsagent or a plane to go to Ibiza. If you have ever run your own business you will know what we mean.

The 4 Hour Work Week by Timothy Ferriss is a great book that talks about using leverage through outsourcing. It certainly gave us a shift in perception and where we were spending our time:

www.progressiveproperty.co.uk/readinglist.asp

The greatest business people in the world understand this concept, because they have head to learn it though experience. If we ever want to grow, or upscale to the next level, whether in business or investing, we need more help. We need more people, and more of other people's money.

Many of the greatest investors never actually use any of their own money but invest millions. Many of the biggest business owners don't work day to day yet employ thousands of people.

In investment terms, relating this concept to Property, leverage is utilising other people's time, money and skills to gain greater advantage, result or wealth than you ever could on your own.

Think of buying a Property now. Do you think you would be able to find it, survey it, do the conveyancing, find a solicitor, organise the mortgage and so on, all on your own?

The more people we can utilise, especially experts in the areas that perhaps we aren't as strong, the better the results we will get.

In Property investment we can look at leverage from two angles:
1. Leveraging other people and their time to gain greater financial benefit.
2. Leveraging the banks' money to earn a greater return.

It is very important to understand that leverage is not using other people; that will end up more expensive in the long term, guaranteed. Remember that cost is not just financial. It can be reputational [did we make that one up too?] So much time can be lost for the future which will equate to pounds and pence, and you will never be able to get it back.

Starting at point no.1, let's look at the best ways to leverage other people for win-win scenarios, and your long term financial gain:

Get other people to do the things you can't. Be a great 'people person' and always offer benefits and value to them. This is as relevant if you have 10 staff as if you just deal with people on a daily basis. Your ability to leverage and attract wealth and success will rely upon you being a relationship expert:

- Never ridicule someone who is learning
- Only reprimand in private and when absolutely necessary
- Always praise good work publicly
- Be personable and care about other people
- Always involve people in your long term vision
- Reward good work financially and in appreciation/praise
- Motivate, inspire and lead by example
- Be consistent
- Forgive
- Be clear of the outcome before you start [write it down]
- Set realistic goals: set others up for success
- Earn respect and keep respect [which may involve distance and professionalism]

You might think that this is not specifically Property related, but some skills are just essential in all areas of life. These relate directly to the way you treat everyone that will be involved in the growing and profitability of your portfolio, and are very important.

**Fundamental tip No.1:
Life is about people and how you make them *feel*. People like and are naturally drawn to people who make them feel good.

Always be thinking in terms of leverage. Every person you meet has the ability to help you to your financial goals. You can help them to theirs. You can help each other. These rules apply not just in your handling of agents and vendors, but in all areas of life.

Make your money and your wealth work for you. If most of it is stuffed under your mattress then it may be going down in value by 5% or more per year. The average inflation figure since 1948 has been 5.8%. More about inflation later but remember this: you could be investing that cash for an infinite return using other people's money. And you can sleep easily!

This takes us to point 2. We believe that you will already be thinking about this, and may have experienced it yourself. As Property investors we like to use as much of the banks' money and as little of our own to earn potentially infinite returns.

A simple Buy to Let mortgage in today's market will require a 15% deposit. Yes there are other mortgage products that allow 90% or more, and there are bridging loans and such that use leverage, and we'll talk about these in forthcoming chapters.

The bank will lend the other 85% of the purchase price needed so that you can buy a given Property. Banks are willing to lend such a great amount on Property [as opposed to shares, bonds and other vehicles] because Property is very secure and stable. The banks know they have a good chance of getting their money back if things go wrong and you cannot keep up repayments, as their loan to you is secured on an historically stable asset.

You will use the money received from your tenant renting out your Property to pay the bank [mortgage] back. Here you have twice effectively used leverage.

This next paragraph is a fundamental piece in the Property investment puzzle:

You will earn your return on the full value of the Property having only paid out 15% of the full price. That is leverage. And that is only the start.

Do you remember just a few moments ago we we're talking about the Law of compounding? This is where leverage really comes into its own.

We discussed the Rule of 72 working on the amount of capital that you invest, and we used the simple example of a £100,000 Property bought for £85,000.

We kept is simple, stating that a deal like this would probably cost you about £3,000 to £5,000.

And we gave you the figures below based on your ROCE [return on capital employed - spent]:

5% growth: 72/5 = 14.4 years to turn £5,000 into £10,000
8% growth: 72/8 = 9 years to turn £5,000 into £10,000
11.74% growth: 72.11.74 = 6 years 48 days to turn £5,000 into £10,000

Using the leverage you can obtain through Property, we can absolutely nail these figures [beat them easily!]

Taking the example of your £100,000 Property, in 10 years at the 3 given growth figures, the results are as follows:

5% growth: £100,000 becomes £162,889
8% growth: £100,000 becomes £215,892
11.74% growth: £100,000 becomes £303,450

So instead of taking between 6 to 14 years to double your cash and get a 200% return, you could be getting an ROCE [return on the cash you spent] of over 4000%. If you want to see exactly how this is worked out, please turn to the back of the book on page 377. If you feel you need to read more to get a better understanding, why not read it when you've finished the book?

We still know many investors who buy Property for cash. They are not effectively utilising leverage and could buy 7 times as much Property for the same money. Just imagine earning 7 times as much money for nothing now...

How would that feel?

Are you sitting on an asset? Think of your own Property now. Over half of the people we regularly speak to at seminars, events, or just in person have enough equity in their home to buy more Property [and earn much more using leverage]. If you or someone you know [perhaps a family member] owns a house, think now how long you have had it; perhaps 2 years, 5 years or more. Think back to what you bought it for; perhaps less than £100,000? Think now to what it is worth. If you don't know, look for what similar properties are selling for on www.nethouseprices.com or www.rightmove.co.uk. You could also get an estate agent to value it for you [if you are even just thinking of selling your home, they will do it for free].

There is a great chance that the value of your home has gone up in value £50,000, £100,000 or more in a very short space of time. In fact, some of our investors' homes doubled in less than 5 years!

Read these next 2 paragraphs carefully. They could be the difference that makes the difference. It could be this alone that helps to secure your long term financial independence and a Property portfolio that will earn for you for life:

You probably have enough equity to buy more Property, get the tenants to pay your mortgages and generate additional equity on perhaps 5-10 properties rather than just your own home. That is what leverage is really about!

Whatever equity you have made on your house now, multiply that by 5 or 10 and imagine what that means to you. Think of £500,000 to £1million now. Imagine 10% of that per year for the rest of your life. Would that help you for your retirement or the lifestyle you desire? Would that give you freedom, choice and independence now?

You can leverage anything: estate agents, leaflets, other people, websites, e-mail marketing systems, joint ventures, we could go on and on. Always be thinking leverage.

At Progressive Property, we effectively leverage the money loaned by the bank to purchase assets for you up to 10 times the value you would be able to achieve with just your own money. Then we leverage evidenced discounts to get your deposit[s] back so that you can buy infinite amounts of Property with one deposit pot. [More later – that's the exciting part!].

You leverage our time and expertise to do this so that you are free to live your own life.

## Summary

Always think of how you can use leverage. How can you earn maximum return on minimum investment and use other people's money for potentially infinite ROI?

Rob Moore & Mark Homer

# Potential pitfalls

Danger danger [don't panic].

There are, as with any kind of investment, potential banana skins that you should be aware of if you want to make your investments work for you [for life].

Believe us when we say that most people, especially companies, will not tell you most of this. We believe in the 'warts and all' approach, because it's all about setting your expectations at the right point and being realistic from the start.

If you know ballpark figures for your investments [purchase costs, maintenance, rentals etc] and what you can realistically expect, then there shouldn't be many flies turning up in your soup. No major surprises; no financial disasters.

We believe the potential pitfalls of investing in Property are as follows [and you should know them before moving forward]:

**War/acts of terrorism/the Taliban/Kamikaze**: yes it seems ridiculous, and yes it probably is, but there is a very slim chance that there could be a major war or other disaster that is not covered by your household insurance!

If there is a war or act of terror, then we're all likely to be hiding in bunkers living on tins of beans and condensed milk, rather than worrying about collecting rent.

Rob Moore & Mark Homer

Ok, so we **are** messing about a little here, but there are paranoid people out there [you know who you are - stop hiding!] and we said that we wanted to cover **everything**.

A '**Market Crash**' this one really gets us both.

If you want to read some specific details about what happens when 'the market is crashing,' when London is burning and when all the rats are running out of town, you can view our second book, 'Make Cash in a Property Market Crash' [it is especially relevant if you want to make money right now], but you must be fast, and this is only for the very serious who really want to make cash in Property:

www.progressiveproperty.co.uk/book2-buy-now.asp

First of all we have to stand up, put our hands in the air and tell you that we didn't go through the 'crash' of the 1980's. We were about 2 years old when that kicked off and we didn't experience it first hand.

So before we go on a rant, let us give you some specific figures about the 'worst time for Property in history.'

That being said, according to www.communities.gov.uk, the market as a whole did not drop through the 80's, as an average. In fact the lowest growth year was 1982 at 2.5% and the highest was 1988 at 25.6%!

In the 90's Property did go down 4 years in a row between 1990 and 1993. The market never went down by more than 3.8% in any one of those 4 years and averaged over 2% per year over the 4 year period [10% less than the market had gone up by in 1989 alone!].

Even in the 80's, the average Property price never actually went down, according to this source. Of course some areas may have been affected more than others, and we are only talking averages. If you went through it you know what you experienced and hopefully the knowledge in this book will help in being prepared for the future.

What we are trying to point out here is that the sensationalist 'crash' was not half as catastrophic as people believe, or as the newspapers reported. It also shows that with a mid – long term holding strategy, one year's growth can wipe out 5 years or more of downward movement, as it easily did.

Remember newspapers are there to sell stories, and that is it. That is how they make their money. We make our money by finding and sharing the truth about Property. They make their money by adding spin and hype to everything with a little pinch of gross sensationalism. That is what sells newspapers.

Have you not noticed in the media that things are either absolutely amazing or verging on disaster? Nothing is ever just normal; nothing is like it is in real life. Celebrities are either 'flavour of the month' or 'dirty love rats' and nothing in between. The media spin around the Property market is no different.

We're absolutely obsessed with Property here in the UK; it's major news, it's all we talk about. It's almost as big as David Beckham's foot bone or Tom Cruises' couch jumping confessions.

This is obviously a good thing. We all want to own Property here; it's the new handbag dog [except it's not new at all]. In other countries, and let's use Germany as an example, Property ownership is far less prevalent; lending criteria is far more stringent and far larger deposits are often needed; many more people therefore rent.

So we must put this into perspective; opportunity is there but what sells papers is not necessarily real. Just imagine what life would be like if we lived by their words. In fact, don't; it's not worth it.

A basic and fundamental rule here: only listen to those who know what they are talking about and can give evidence to backup their knowledge. You wouldn't give your baby to a butcher, so don't leave your investment decisions in the hands of journalists, or people who don't really know what they're doing.

So history tells us that markets go up on average rather nicely and can drop a little [though only 4 years out of the last 57], but it is something to be aware of. It should not scare you. It should not put you off buying Property. There are so many people who we speak to who are still waiting to say 'I told you so' when the market crashes. They have been waiting 10 years and missed out on complete financial independence in that time.

The knotted ol' grumpy fools [bless their hearts]! Surely we should want each other to succeed rather than fail? Don't wait to buy Property, buy Property and wait. In times of market downturn, skilled investors will make money. Skilled investors will make money regardless of the marketplace.

Whilst the market is 'bull' and riding high many of us who have a good portfolio will experience healthy capital growth and benefit from this increase in the value of our Property. When the market goes south, the average punter panics and wants to sell immediately, taking a hit on any losses gained. This is blindness and it is at this time that the savvy investor can pick up properties at discounted prices, thus making his or her profit from day one in equity; immediately at purchase.

Either way the educated investor wins. The sheep get skinned and lose their wool and are left out in the cold; going baa. We shall discuss this more later.

It is this simple; don't sell your Property in a downturn [if there ever is another one]. Hold it rented out, and let it regain its value and rise again; because it will. *Think long term*.

Rob Moore & Mark Homer

Rents actually firmed up when the market 'slowed' in the 80's and early 90's. So many people were in negative equity [many did not follow the rules and buy at evidenced discount – otherwise they would have had a buffer. Some could have been unlucky, but we don't really believe in luck] and couldn't afford to buy, so they rented, and the demand for rental properties increased.

This kind of scenario is not always the best news for first time buyers, but investors will do very well in this situation. You should be considering yourself an investor by now.

This is the basis on which all of the successful [£5million+] Property investors that we have met have developed their strategy.

**Big nasty interest rate rises**: now this one we do have to watch, as many people will tell you who were around when the interest rates almost tripled overnight [or so my Dad recalls! - Rob].

This is one of the biggest fears [common of course; it's hardly popular] of the investors we help and talk to, especially following press reports, and the creeping up of interest rates over 2007.

Firstly, we don't really see the interest rates going too high for the near future. This is what most serious commentators who are experts in their field tell us. Perhaps the lows of about 4.5% weren't realistic for the long term and we should be grateful if we got mortgages fixed at that time.

Of course, this is what is happening currently. The fact is that interest rates will change; they may come down in the near future as a calming effort after the credit crunch, but that may only be short term. If you want to get an idea of what interest rates may do over the long term, you can look at www.swap-rates.com.

This looks at the future predictions of interest rates based on LIBOR rates, base rates, Euribor rates, Gilt rates, Historic rates and trends. Don't worry if most of those don't mean a thing, it's just a useful tool to look ahead and see where the experts think the interest rates could be going.

That aside, it's really quite simple, straightforward and sensible to think about fixing your mortgage rates on your properties. You can get competitive 10 year fixed rate mortgages at the moment that can actually work out to be cheaper than some variable rate mortgages. We will go into this in much more detail later. This is the most effective way of allaying fears when it comes to potential interest rate rises, and has you protected no matter what happens.

Isn't that comforting to know? Well actually, it is just sensible.

Of course with every change comes opportunity, and remember as stated earlier, you can profit very nicely by helping people out of debt when the interest rates rise. You can buy their

Rob Moore & Mark Homer

properties from them before they get repossessed. You can even rent it back to them so you don't have to find a tenant. Can you see how good this is? More later.

In order to get a 'crash' we would normally need to see 2 economic changes rather than, for example, just a big interest rate rise. A secondary factor such as a sharp rise in unemployment would [according to many experts] also need to take place. Neither is currently forecasted by serious commentators for the foreseeable future.

And of course as serious Property investors we will adapt and change to the market, and find ways to profit whatever the market is doing, won't we?

## Summary

Know and beware of potential pitfalls before you invest. Be realistic, do your diligence and set your expectations at the right level. Know that you are the one in control, and that most people don't have enough knowledge to be taken too seriously. Once you have made your choices and you're happy: take immediate action. Procrastination is a disease.

# The Property buying process

Later on in this book we'll go over many of the processes of buying a Property in much more detail. You may learn some useful secrets in transforming the performance of your existing portfolio [or saving time and money when starting to build it].

For now, see the processes you will need to understand and go through as a serious Property investor when buying a Property below. Not all of them will always apply, but knowing all of this in advance will save you a hell of a lot of time, pain and money:

**Decide how much you want to invest**: do you have equity in your Property? Do you have savings or other investments? Have you sold a business or taken redundancy? The amount of capital you have to invest will determine your strategy.

We shall go over this in more detail later in the book. It will be absolutely essential for you to create your own set of 'rules,' determined primarily by your goals [we all have different desired outcomes] if you want to make consistent money from Property investment.

The single biggest mistake that speculators and gamblers make that holds them back from true investor status is that they buy without having a set of rules. In effect, they don't know what they are buying and how their 'investment' will turn out.

By the end of this book you will have a clear idea of how your rules will look like to you, and what they will mean for you [as long as you follow and apply all that you are reading now].

And they'll change as you go on. They should; and that's good. You will be improving all the time.

**Decide on your area**: we shall discuss the process of diligence to identify your area later in the book. For now just know that you should be sticking to a specific, local area.

**Decide on your Property type**: most people find Property by accident, or are lured by new build and off plan 'developers' discounts' and such like. There is diligence that should be carried out to find the best type of investment for you, which shall be revealed later.

**How are you going to find your Property?** Are you going to use estate agents and build relationships? Drop leaflets in the right areas and to the right properties? Will you set up a website and advertise using Google Adwords [or other CPC/PPC engines], affiliates and internet marketing?

**Do *ALL* the figures on your desired properties**: this should be done at this stage and no later. Have you thought about all the costs; and we mean *all* the costs. All will be revealed and prepare to be surprised [especially if you have bought from some new build companies in the past].

**Find a good mortgage broker**: this is vital for investors as specific mortgage products are often required. They may also refer you to a good solicitor. More explained later.

**Get a decision in principle [D.I.P] for a mortgage**: most investors leave this too late. You must have this in place to save hassle, grief, and be in a position to buy fast. Many agents may ask you this when you enquire about properties with them.

**View the Property**: always view the Property. Does it need refurbishment work? Check for damp. Check the windows [old windows can be expensive to replace] and check the boiler. Check the surrounding area. Check.

**Make offers on the properties you have sourced**: how are you going to negotiate your desired price and how are you going to know that the price is of genuine value? Always make offers. If you don't ask; you don't get [thanks Dad!]. Remember it is a numbers game and you'll get some deals that you really didn't expect to get, and some that will surprise you [at how good they are]. Offer on everything structurally sound and offer low.

**Get a survey of the Property**: this must be done to ascertain the value for mortgage lending purposes. Whether you do this before you offer or after is up to you. Remember that it can be expensive to get surveys done too early if vendors then pull out. The more diligence you do, the better equipped you'll be.

**Find a tenant/letting agent**: most people leave this very late and it costs them heavily. Start looking as early as you can and you'll save money. Managing tenants yourself can be grief and we just don't bother with it. Get a good agent to do it for you; it's their job [remember leverage]. You don't want to be paying mortgage payments because your Property is empty, do you? Use a letting agent and pay their fees, it will end up saving you time and money in the mid-long term. Remember, you must find a good one.

**Agree a price**: make an offer and agree a price. Once you do this and you're happy *never* pull out, especially if you are building relationships with estate agents. This is so so important. Don't even think about it! Of course, if you have followed the steps here you will never need to pull out of a purchase, will you?

**Find a good solicitor for conveyancing and legal work**: there are specific legal requirements to purchasing a Property; you'll need to find a good solicitor. We know some good ones and some not so good ones, and we're happy to pass you the details of the good ones. Most will seem quite efficient at first but the service can very often tail off.

**Full mortgage application**: your broker will arrange this with you. A good one will make the process quick and easy. A bad one will take 6 months and make out that it is very difficult to get a mortgage unless you can prove you earn over £50,000. If you need a good one then we can help you. They're not that easy to find.

**Pay your deposit over**: required to receive the mortgage.

**Exchange on the Property**: once application and legal work are completed and relevant fees are paid, then contracts are exchanged, at which time it is too late to pull out.

**Complete any refurbishment work**: [we are assuming that you have good tradesmen at your disposal. Don't get your hands dirty here, this is not Property ladder]. Start this as soon as you can after exchange to save time on your mortgage payments [which have not started yet]. Start earlier and your work could be in vain if the vendor pulls out. Start too late and you could pay extra mortgage payments while the Property is empty.

**Check your costs**: you should be keeping a good eye on these so that they don't spiral out of control. The quicker you are, the more efficient you are, and the better team you have around you, the less any deal will cost you.

**Complete on the Property**: drawdown of funds. Your mortgage payments start now. You can house your tenant and complete any work to make the Property habitable.

**Pay your insurances** and gas safety checks [and perhaps even council tax for long refurb work]: We all have to do it.

**House your tenant**: make sure you have an AST [Assured Shorthold Tenancy Agreement] signed between you and your tenant. The letting agent should have vetted your tenant and arranged this.

**Set up a separate portfolio account**: money flies all over the place in Property investment so we recommend opening a separate account. Automate all payments in and out through D.D if you can.

**Get your Property revalued**: if you are finding discounts and using the tools that we teach in this book then you will be getting your deposits back. You will probably need a different surveyor around to value your Property this time as you will require a higher valuation.

**Organise your remortgage**: just like you did your first one.

Receive your deposit back and find your next Property with the same deposit funds: Be patient!

And that is just the start...

# Summary

The best way to sum up this chapter is to read it again!

# Have a Property wealth strategy

## Define what wealth means to you

Wealth means completely different things to each and every one of us. Mother Teresa's definition of wealth is probably a little different from that of Bill Gates, and again probably a little different from yours or ours.

Wealthy investors know exactly what they want when it comes to wealth. It really doesn't matter what it is, and how much it is, as long as you are happy with it and it will give you the life of your choice. Your strategy that you create is personal to you, and will come down to what you want for your life and the lives of those closest to you.

Think now, before you read on, about what you want for your life. Not yet but in a moment. We are not setting your Property wealth strategy in stone just yet, we have just started. Knowing that you are thinking about what you want as you read this book will help you formalise it later, once you have finished.

What benefits do you want? What do you want your portfolio for? What is it that you want money and wealth for?

Why do we buy a car? Not just to sit in the garage or to polish on the driveway, but to actually drive it and take us from A. to B. Maybe it is to carry work tools around? Maybe it is to pick up girls or play fat bass in McDonald's car park?

Rob Moore & Mark Homer

Do you want wealth to change the world? To create a higher standard of living for you and the ones you love? Do you want to set up a shelter or charity? Do you want to leave a legacy? Do you want the latest golf club or to travel to Outer Mongolia? Do those matching shoes and handbags have your name written all over them?

This is your vision; your big picture, and this needs to be thought about **before** you chunk down to your set of Rules. Your rules should provide for your life, just like your business should provide the lifestyle you want. Most people forget why they even started business and end up being a slave.

Do you want 5 properties? 10 properties? 200 properties? Do you want passive income of £50,000 per year, tax free? Do you want more? Do you want a portfolio that you can retire on? Are you 28 or 58? [Or any other age for that matter].

This will all impact upon your personal strategy. You'll hear this word quite a lot, and most people, if we are honest, don't really understand what it means:

"A careful plan or method : a clever stratagem b : the art of devising or employing plans or stratagems toward a goal"

That is the dictionary definition. Notice the words 'art' and 'plan' and 'goal' in there. These are very important and specific. We would also add that anything accidental or not planned is also a strategy; just an ineffective one!

Do you want to leave your children with a large portfolio that can fund their retirement or a big nasty inheritance tax bill?! Do you want to be a full time investor or do you want someone to do it for you? Do you want to work again? Do you want to travel?

We could go on.

Think about how much you are prepared to invest. Do you have equity in your Property that you can leverage [explained later]? Do you want to invest a percentage on an ongoing basis? Your attitude to risk may be dependent on certain factors such as age, experience and number of dependents.

Perhaps you might even want to write your thoughts down as you think about them now. This is very important indeed. Any goal, value, idea or concept should be written down. Have a particular folder or file for your personal goals and keep them safe where only you know where they are.

We have provided some space at the back of this book for you to do exactly that should you wish. It might be a good idea to write them down now, in this book, so that you have everything in once place.

Turn to page 371 and fill in the questions provided.

This is your confidential information. Use it as a reference, a guide, a rulebook, a checklist, a diary, a goal and as a useful tool to look back on to see just how much progress you have made.

## See your journey before you

We really believe in the Law of attraction; a glorified Law of focus. You get what you focus on, think about the most and attract into your life.

We have read hundreds of 'amazing' stories on the law of attraction; and we know that everyone has an inspiring story to tell. It is our belief that we get things in life to the extent in which we believe we will. You might want to re-read that sentence now and think very carefully about it; it could be one of the most important things you learn.

We have had many discussions about the 'law of attraction' especially since 'the secret' brought it into the public eye. Some swear by it, some believe that it is magic, Deepak Chopra thinks you can make it happen doing nothing but meditating and dropping a 'seed of intention' into 'the gap', Tony Robbins thinks you take 'massive action' seeking 'constant and never ending improvement' until you make your dreams a reality. It's up to you what you decide is your reality and how you decide to make this information work for you. The following stories are my personal experiences [Rob]. Some think it's voodoo; some think it's magic, some think it's attraction, some think it's being open to opportunity, some think it's co-incidence, some think it's luck, some think it's bullshit.

Remember this; you have the choice; so why not choose beliefs that give you the best chance of success? Why would you do anything else?

In 2006 I went to Australia to do a seminar presentation course with one of the world's leading NLP and personal development trainers. I made the decision less than 1 week before the course started so I knew I had to get cracking with booking the flights and hotels and selling my boss on why he should pay nearly £5,000 for me to spend 2 weeks off work.

This was all fairly straightforward as I really wanted to do the course, but one rather large obstacle did face me 3 days before I was about to leave; I couldn't find my passport. And I really couldn't. You know when you've looked so hard that you start looking in the same place for the fifth time trying to convince yourself that you haven't looked there yet? That's where I was.

I went to the passport office in Peterborough and they weren't budging on a 7 day timeframe to get me a new passport. I offered to drive to Liverpool where they make them, pay double, triple, I probably begged on my knees and may have even tried to bribe the cashiers with lunch and flowers and compliments and a ride in my then new 350Z and whatever else I could think of.

Nothing was going to work. But I was convinced that I was still going to Australia.

So I went to bed the night before I was due to leave, and everyone in our office knew that I didn't have my passport, so I guess they thought I would be in the office the next day to work. And as I slept that night I had a dream. It was as clear and real as any dream I have had, where my passport has fallen down the back of my filing cabinet and got lodged behind the files at the bottom and to the back. Somewhere where you would never ever find it, no matter how hard you looked.

I went in to work the next day, not having remembered the dream but still looking for the passport. Our PA at the time asked if I had looked in the filing cabinet and I snapped that I had emptied it no less than 6 times...

And then I just knew, and remembered the dream, and frantically picked up and shook the filing cabinet. Sure enough, last to fall out on top of all the files and papers that were strewn across the floor was my passport. Joy.

My Dad has had 2 very clear dreams of horses that would win the Grand National. Now I don't know how many dreams he has had about horses and races, but I remember the day when he won £7,000 on Rough Quest on a dream he had the night before. I was 17 at the time, and that was a lot of money to thrown on a 'hunch.' Of course, my Dad didn't see it that way, but I've never got a real explanation as to what he thought the dream was, or how it happened, or what it meant.

And to be honest I don't really care. I don't need all the answers. Mark does, and we often talk about what we believe the Law of attraction really is. He can't accept anything mystical, magical, mysterious or anything hoodoo voodoo, he has to have a scientific explanation for it. It has to be focus, co-incidence and opportunity aligning.

I'm pretty happy with that reasoning. It works for me in my life because I can control the things I want for my life and with that explanation I can make things happen. However there is a little in me that likes to believe that we don't know everything, and that there is something more powerful that helps us attract what we want through energy transfer or whatever. I don't need the explanation, I have the evidence and I'm happy that I can continue to use it to achieve more in my life.

We're not telling you what to believe, who the hell are we to do that? We just want to show you what we've seen in our experience, and what we have seen get results time and time again. The choice is yours. The reason and the explanation are yours. The decision is yours.

So you know all about this because this is not the first time you have heard it. Not just in this book but in the 'Real World' too. If you want to read the Secret you can buy it from our website at

www.progressiveproperty.co.uk/readinglist.asp

in the personal development section of our Amazon aStore.

Rob Moore & Mark Homer

Now it is time to really make this work for you. If you want to be successful in Property you need to have the skill of seeing your journey before you. This involves the following process:

## Where are you now?

You absolutely must know where you are starting from. Of course this sounds ridiculously obvious. There are many people out there who could be described as 'delusional' when it comes to knowing where they are. We've all been there. Now it's time for us to get real. Honestly evaluate where you are [wherever it is, is just right for you] and get excited about the path you are about to build.

Again, we have a section at the back of the book for you to write this down. Simply turn to page 372.

Know your exact financial position to the penny: your monthly expenses, budgets and cash flow. Know the assets and liabilities [debt] you have and know your net worth. Your total net worth will be your marker for your wealth and your progress; it is *not* just about cash-flow.

## Know where you want to go: your goal

You must have a clear idea of where you want to be, as discussed earlier. Of course your goal will be individual to you; we are all driven by different things. It will grow and evolve; it is just at the very start now. Your goals *will* change, and that is fine. We know that life is a journey and not a destination, and each major goal will act as a significant milestone in your life.

When you refer back to this section and define your strategy you must quantify your end goal: be specific with timescales, numbers and figures. The more real, tangible and specific you can make your goals, the more likely you are to attract them. Be the man or woman with the plan: have a strategy.

The reason that the majority of investors are in financial slavery is not because they don't have the ability to make or attract money; there are many people who make millions per year and are still broke. It is the lack of a specific plan and strategy. They don't have their rules in place, or at least they don't stick to them. Many buy Property all over the place. We personally know an investor who bought 87 properties, all with good and genuine existing discounts, yet went bankrupt because they were all over the country and he just couldn't manage them].

Many do not focus and get a little greedy or go too quickly. If I [Rob] had bought 50 properties in my first year, as was my goal, I would never have coped; financially or emotionally.

However, I still got nearly half the way there, so the goal was well worth putting out there, don't you think?

Remember the more specific you can be when you design your own personal strategy, the better. It may change, so be it; that is life. In your journey you will make many changes now and you will evolve like you never have before. For now, just make the plan.

And that's exactly what you are doing now, isn't it?

In seeing your journey before you remember the following very important points:

It is *never* too late to start planning, investing in Property and becoming wealthy. Start now, get perfect later.

Of course analysis is important, but analysis paralysis is just as bad [if not worse]. If you run head first into a brick wall without a helmet at least you will have started, and you'll learn a different strategy for breaking through it [that will not hurt quite as much!].

We bought a couple of kippers [bad investment properties!] when we first started, and of course they look silly now, but the lessons we got buying them by just going for it were so fundamental in getting us where we are now.

Colonel Sanders is a great example. KFC Inc was formed in the late 1950's when 'Colonel Sanders' was nearly 70. We once helped an investor who was 76 get a Buy to Let investment Property. Age is *not* an excuse. Don't even think about excuses! Excuses are the stories that people who fail tell to make themselves feel better. The best and most fruitful, rich, loving and exciting years of your life could be the ones you still have left, and you could live until you are 105!

You are **never too young** to invest and educate yourself to become very wealthy either. There are many great entrepreneurs who are in their teens. The million dollar homepage that generated $1million was created by Alex Tew at 21 and Facebook CEO Mark Zuckerberg was only 20 when he created the infamous social networking site.

**NOW** is always the best time.

Or let us ask you this question:

When is now the best time to start investing?

There are 1000's of opportunities out there each and every day. Seeing your path before you opens your awareness to the things that you need, the people you need to meet [and work with] and the challenges you need to overcome to get where you want to be. Know that they will only present themselves to you if you are looking.

And remember the difference between investment, speculation and gambling. The last two are for poor people.

Your strategy is your road map, which if you follow and update when necessary, will lead you straight to your apple tree with those juicy golden apples...

Rob Moore & Mark Homer

Your strategy should be reviewed yearly as should your finances. Don't be scared of those spreadsheets, get them open, update them and do a financial check up to see where you are. Compare them to last year and see that you are making progress in the right direction.

The good news: if you've been reading this whole section and thinking 'yes, yes, ok, good; but I don't even know where to start;' then fear not. All will become clear.

If you already have a strategy, then be excited that you could save yourself years of time and £1,000's of pounds just by reading this book.

We really could go through strategy after strategy [there are 1000's just in the Property world] but we're not going to do that to you. We have built our wealth and our business on **one** strategy. **One strategy only.** As will become clear, there really are 1,000's of opportunities out there when we look for them, and one of the hardest things in Property investing is knowing which one to use; and then stick with and focus on.

This strategy is easy to follow, easy to implement and anyone can do it, unlike many other complicated strategies out there. Simply add in your personal goals and make this strategy work for you, because you really can.

We have placed our Property buying strategy at the back of the book for you to look over and help you with yours. Remember that our goals may be very different to yours, so use it as an example only and build upon it to tailor it to help you achieve all that you want from your portfolio that will help you to your goals and big picture vision.

Go to page 375 any time you feel like it.

## Summary

Know what wealth means to you and what you want from your portfolio. Know where you are, where you want to be and see your journey before you. Be specific and have a strategy. Use the Law of Attraction and make your goals a reality now. Take the strategy in this book and you can have all the wealth you want, it is your choice.

Rob Moore & Mark Homer

# Interest only vs. repayment

This one sparks a great debate and thus warrants its very own section.

Many of you will know that nearly all investment mortgages are interest only, rather than capital repayment: you are only paying off the interest on the loan rather than the loan itself.

Stay with us here. It is when most people understand the advantages of this concept that everything seems to fit into place.

The average repayment loan [mortgage] will take you 25 years to pay off. When you do eventually pay it off you will have paid off around 2.5 times the value of your Property. Yes you will own your Property outright, but for a £100,000 Property you will have paid roughly £250,000 for it after the 25 years [at the time of writing, depending on interest rates]. That is a lot of tied up capital that could have been invested, leveraged and making you much more money.

As you will probably know; this is known as 'cost of capital.' A great example is the purchase of a car. Many people will tell you it's foolish to get a car on finance; and we certainly don't believe in stretching yourself into debt to buy 'liabilities.'

Example: let's make the assumption that you can easily afford a car costing £25,000; cash or finance.

*Option 1:* You buy it on finance. You tie up a £5,000 deposit and raise the rest through finance, costing you approx £425 per month on a repayment loan for 60 months depending on interest rates. You have £20,000 to invest.

*Option 2:* You buy it cash. You have zero repayments and zero cash to invest.

*Option 1:* You invest the £20,000 and with it, using your increasing knowledge, you can plausibly buy 1 Property per year with the same capital. For ease of figures; these properties are worth £100,000 based on today's figures.

Compounded equity at end of yr 5 [based on 5% growth]: **£168,461**

Go to the back of the book to page 379 if you would like to see how we arrive at this figure in more detail.

*Option 1:*
Money made: £168,461
Money spent on repayments: £425 x60 = £25,500
Total: **£142,961**

*Option 2:* You save the £425 per month repayments and it takes 47 months to accrue £20,000 to invest. This leaves around 1 year to invest. You invest the £20,000 and buy 1 equivalent Property for £121,550 [£100,000 Property + 4 years growth].

Equity at end of year 5 [or year 1 for this strategy]: £24,309

*Option 2:*
Money made: £24,309
Money spent on repayments: 0
Total: £24,309

Interesting, isn't it?!

A couple of additional points: in 25 years you would have paid off your mortgage, all set at the current rate [i.e. inflation: the value of money]. In 25 years all of that money that you have paid towards your repayment mortgage will actually be worth much less than what you paid for it relatively. The £250,000 could have actually gone down in value by almost three-quarters if the rate of inflation stays relatively high as it is.

Quick aside: Don't be fooled by 'official inflation figures.' The actual rate of inflation can be [are] much higher. In our current economic conditions the price of food, commodities, petrol and general living are on the way up, alarmingly so, far more than the government may openly admit.

Taxes are on the way up; we are getting fined for everything we do. Our solicitor got fined £40 for putting out a cigarette by a 'community support officer,' Rob got fined £60 because SatNav took him momentarily in a 'congestion zone,' Mark get's parking tickets when he is loading stuff into the office. They want to fine us at our local council for putting rubbish in the wrong coloured bin and charge us a new tax to collect it – we're just waiting for breathing tax!

And guess what: wages are not going up anywhere near in relative terms to this. End of rant.

We can actually work the impact inflation will have almost exactly using the 'rule of 70.' It is like using the rule of 72 in reverse, and is a quick way of working out the time in which it will take the value of money to halve, knowing the figure of inflation.

Picking up on the example on the previous page of £250,000, to determine the time for money's buying power to halve, simply divide the "rule-quantity" [70] by the inflation rate. Let's look at some examples:

Inflation @ 2%: 70/2 = 35 years for £250,000 to ½ in value
Inflation @ 4%: 70/4 = 17.5 years for £250,000 to ½ in value
Inflation @ 6%: 70/6 = 11.67 for £250,000 to ½ in value

20 years ago properties could be bought for around £5,000 as many of you will know. £5,000 doesn't even buy a garage now! Can you see how easy it would be to pay off £5,000 now that your house is worth around £200,000?! If you buy a house for £200,000 today and inflation stays relatively consistent to the last 20 years, then that £200,000 could be worth, in relative terms, what £5,000 is today. Don't worry if this is not clear, we'll run over it again.

We'll discuss in just a second why most people will never actually get to the end of their repayment term; another reason for taking out interest only mortgages.

So the second point about capital repayment mortgages: they are not set so that you pay equal amounts of interest to repayment on a monthly basis [as you might expect]. Because mortgage companies are in the business of making money, because the market is so competitive and they know you'll be with another lender in 3 years, they make their loans 'top heavy.'

This means that for the first few years of your repayment mortgage you are paying off nearly all interest and very little capital. It is not until you get right near the end of your 25 [+] year term that you are paying off a decent amount of capital. This is the lenders' way of getting maximum money out of you in a minimum period of time.

This brings us to the next point. They arrange the loans like this for profit. That goes without saying. Because the market is so competitive and transient, the lenders know that in 2-3 years you are likely to have remortgaged and changed mortgages in the search for a better rate or to release cash from your equity. People rarely stay with the same mortgage company for very long nowadays.

In short you are spending so much of your available [investible - made up word again perhaps?] capital on a repayment mortgage which is just going down in value over time. It makes far more sense to invest that money and compound the returns, and let it go up and up and up.

Let's do some maths on this shall we? This part is fun and it's very powerful. Let's just take that £150,000 that you save by taking an interest only mortgage on a £100,000 house; to keep it simple. An average monthly repayment based on these figures [depending on interest rates] would be £833.33.

You decide to invest £50,000 of that repayment you have saved, every 5 years [£833.33 x 12 x 5 = £49,999.80 – you put up the extra 20p!] You know, or at least you will by the end of the book, that you can buy up to 5 properties with that £50,000.

In 25 years using this simple strategy, you will have bought 15 properties. The total value of those properties using conservative growth figures of 8% would be **£11,813,649**!

That's over **£10million** from one simple strategy. That £100,000 that you still owe on your original house shouldn't be a problem to you now, should it?!

For the exact figures of that calculation go to page 381.

So as you can see there is a huge cost of capital [cost of not investing] involved in paying back a mortgage. This is a fundamental concept for investing. If you have money tied up in your house it could be costing you *millions* by *not* investing it.

And at this point you might be nodding and think yes, it's all very well, but I don't actually own my Property do I?

Well no you don't. But would you rather have 16 properties [yours plus 15 investments] or one, bearing in mind what we are learning here?

And let's look at your end result in 25 years and address this question: in 25 years your £100,000 Property that you bought will still carry a debt of £100,000. Because you have chosen an interest only mortgage, you will still owe that on your Property. Think back to what we said about inflation and the ever decreasing [relative] value of money. In 25 years the £100,000 that you still owe will actually only be worth about a quarter [relatively] of that at that time. The average figure of inflation over the last 59 years has been 5.8%. A good source for this kind of information is www.statistics.gov.uk

However your asset, on current growth figures, is now worth around £800,000 at the end of the 25 years and still has a small loan [chopped down by inflation] that you need to pay off. Do you think you might be able to afford it with the assets just in this one house?!

And what about the other 15 you bought [using the concept of leverage] because you did not have to repay the loan? All of those will also be worth around £800,000 [each].

This is where leverage really comes into its own. The figures are quite breathtaking wouldn't you agree? And remember that you can take all of this growth incrementally if you remortgage [and not pay a penny of tax on it!]. So to keep with this example, you could potentially access 85% of [£100,000 x 15] + 25 year's growth. That could be **£10million** all from the money you would have tied up paying off your first mortgage!

Now we're talking [and we don't use exclamations lightly!].

## Summary:

Remembering leverage and the Law of compounding, keep your investment mortgages to interest only. Invest saved capital and leverage up to 12000% [120 times] over 25 years to secure your financial future.

# Due diligence

Diligence is vital when going into any investment. Due preparation and research should be undertaken [or undertaken for you utilising someone else who knows how to do it].

In Property there are the following factors that need to be considered, planned for, researched, and contingencies put in place for potential worst case scenarios:

- Market conditions
- Interest rates and economic growth
- Demographic and your area to invest
- Location
- Property size
- Property type
- Property condition and potential refurbishment
- Property valuation
- Finance nuances
- Comparable prices
- Cost of repayments
- Running cost of Property with contingencies
- Remortgage strategy
- Demographic and lifetime value of tenant
- Tenant management
- Growth strategy
- Competition
- Other things we may not have thought about from the start

Rob Moore & Mark Homer

This appears quite a lot, doesn't it?

We shall go into much more detail for you as we move through the book. At this point if you would like to see an example of the kind of diligence you should be performing for your area and Property type [which gets easier the more you do it], you can log on to the following website address:

www.progressiveproperty.co.uk/downloads/Progressive-Market-Analysis.pdf

We know this seems a lot. Believe us it does become second nature the more you buy. It is so so important.

**Fundamental tip No.2:
Remember balance is so important. Diligence is important but analysis paralysis is a disease of progress. Do your diligence, take fast and decisive action and get perfect later:

The reduction of risk is proportionate to your increasing of knowledge.

# Summary

Be diligent. Plan, prepare and research carefully. Know what you are buying, reduce the risk and be wary if you are offered Property without due diligence.

# Don't read the papers

Absolutely one of the worst things that we can do as investors is read the papers.

We know how celebrities feel now when there are hundreds of things written about them. Don't get us wrong, we're not celebrities, but there is so much unfounded information out there, it can send us in a spin.

The people who write articles for the newspapers do not have the same agenda that we do. They do not have the same agenda that real Property experts do.

Let's get back to that in a minute. Of course you will know that it is absolutely vital that you read, study and learn from those who have done it if you want to become a successful and profitable Property investor. So you should.

And here is a brief list of the resources that we have found to be accurate and educated. For a more detailed list you can find our resources guide at:

www.progressiveproperty.co.uk/latestpropertynews.asp

The Land registry for sold Property prices
The Economist for economic analysis
The Financial Times for economic news

Rob Moore & Mark Homer

The Communities and Local Government website for housing data

The Halifax, Nationwide and Rightmove for house price data
The commentators for these publications and websites are knowledgeable on the subjects on and around Property, and base their news on facts rather than sensationalism.

Newspaper editors and journalists are trying to sell newspapers. They create stories. Have you noticed the 'lift them up chop them down' attitude our press seem to have? Life is not really like the way it is depicted in many of these publications. Life is not all about the extremes; very often we simply tick along without too much happening of newsworthy note. You know, life as it *really* is.

The papers would be out of business if they did not hype and spin everything. Their stories are often 3, 4 or 5 steps removed from the truth or the actual event that took place. That is their business, but Property is not. We have, on numerous occasions, seen in the same day in the same newspaper that the market was both 'going to crash' and was 'booming.'

This phenomenon has gone wild as of late, with the Property market changing over the last few months. We go into specific detail about the implication of the 'Crash sensation' and the 'Sheople' in our second book, because it is very pertinent at the moment, and this book is designed to be more topical [and shocking]. You can read how this is actually a great thing for us investors here:

www.progressiveproperty.co.uk/book2-buy-now.asp

Stick to the reputable sources and avoid the rest. Especially take with a pinch of salt 'pub talk' where all the apparent experts on Property hangout drinking their pints of bitter shandy. Where do most people who have an opinion about Property get their information [crash-crash- boom-should-have-bought-10-years-ago-it's-all-about-to-crash]? You got it, the newspapers.

## Summary

Only listen to the Property experts. Don't take the newspapers seriously; their agenda is to sell newspapers. [Pub] talk is cheap. Do your diligence using reputable sources and make your own decisions.

# Why 95% of people get it wrong

Don't be a sheep.

If we do what everyone else does then we'll get the same result as everyone else.

Unfortunately the statistics are not good. Most people **are not** wealthy, financially independent or in a position of choice in their life. Out of every 100 people by the age of 65: 25 will be dead, 20 will have incomes of less than £5,000 [no kidding!], 51 will have incomes of less than £17,000, 4 will have incomes over £17,000 and only 1 will be a millionaire.

Most people who try Property don't do anywhere near as well as they could; or perhaps should. Most people will make money in the very long term but they rely on Property [and good old father time] looking after them, rather than getting it right and making serious money through strategy. Most people are living in effect rather than at cause [they are a slave] and they do not know what to do about it. Property does not owe us a living.

You do and you can [for you].

Most people will be happy to tell you what to do with your money and to not buy Property because the market is going to crash any day now. If we follow the statistics that alone should tell us that most of that advice would not be of benefit to us [unless we want to be like the other sheep – 'sheople']. Baa?

Rob Moore & Mark Homer

[And what does 'crash' mean anyway?].

It is very important to be strong and to stick to your strategy that you are now formulating in your mind. Question the advice you're getting from someone, especially if it is the typical 'pub talk' scenario, or words taken straight from a daily tabloid.

When there is a Property 'crash' the 'sheople' flock and they sell and they lose money. The ones who succeed are the ones who have a strategy, are confident in that strategy [and themselves]; the ones who buy and hold when everyone else is selling. It is exactly the same on the stock market, or in business.

Those who are successful are very often quirky, individual, different, sometimes excluded, sometimes ridiculed, very often creative, individual, perhaps stubborn and focused, definitely courageous, mature, educated, experienced, open minded and don't often do what people expect them to do. The rest stay with the herd because it is comfortable [and go baa].

People can also be like crabs. Crab fishermen leave the lid off the boxes that they put crabs in because they know that when a crab tries to get out of the box all the other crabs grab hold with their big claws and pull the crab that dares to venture back into the box.

Be successful, be courageous; don't be a sheep [or a crab].

Don't chase the glitz and the get rich quick. If it looks too good to be true then chances are it is. If you are being offered to become a millionaire in 5 minutes while you sleep [or even anything less than 5-10 years], then be very very suspicious.

Trust your instincts here. You know in your heart what is right and what is not. So many investors we have met are changing tack every 5 minutes; chasing MLM [multi level marketing] schemes without working at the previous one or being lured by inflated prices, false discounts, cash-backs and no money deals.

We shall go into more detail about this later and be specific about what you should watch out for. Be wary, be suspicious and do your diligence.

The biggest investors have built their wealth steadily over time. Many have portfolios generations old and continue to use strategies that have worked for them. 40% of the Times Rich List have done just that.

## Summary

Be strong, be focused and prepare to take some stick from those who don't know what you know. Continue to refine your strategy without getting lured by all that glitters and make your own decisions; don't be a sheep.

Rob Moore & Mark Homer

# Take action: Start Now

**Decision.**

**Fundamental tip No.3:
Start Now. Get perfect later.

Where have we heard that before?!

Perhaps one of the biggest things that we have seen that stops people making forward progress in their lives is procrastination. It is the disease of momentum. Both indecision and over analysis essentially lead to the same thing: a long and windy road to nowhere:

'I want to wait to see what the market is doing.'

'I don't have enough money yet.'

'I don't have enough time.'

We are all going to make mistakes. This is a fact of life, and one that, when we accept this as part of our journey, makes achievement much more accessible [and enjoyable].

A great friend of ours likes to make as many mistakes as he can up front because he believes that the more mistakes he makes the closer to his goal he is getting. We really admire that attitude. Pride and ego are some of the biggest barriers to success. Enjoy listening, enjoy learning and growing, and know that we can all learn something from everyone. Do not fear the consequences of your decisions. Be decisive. Use your knowledge, use your experience, use your intuition; make quick and well informed decisions...

About what you believe. If you don't know, make a guess. You'll be close, and refine it from there. Wealthy people do not wait to make decisions; they make decisions and then refine their strategy and improve upon it.

Do not underestimate the knowledge you already have regardless of where you are in your Property investing career.

**Fundamental tip No.4:
There is a saying in Property that goes: 'Don't wait to buy Property, buy Property and wait.'

Perhaps you have thought about investing, saving or putting money into Property for many years now but have not 'got around to it.' That wouldn't be the first time we have heard that. If we had just a pound for every time we heard that then we would not need to build a portfolio!

Indecision can cost us thousands of pounds and far worse: freedom or happiness. As Napoleon Hill puts it: 'Do not wait; the time will never be "just right." Start where you stand, and work with whatever tools you may have at your command, and better tools will be found as you go along.' We concur!

Remember this very important fact. You will never be 100% ready to start in Property. We weren't; no one is. It's just like having a baby. You can go to the doctors and see the scans, you can go to breathing classes, you can eat all the right foods, do incantations and play dolphin music. You can get a pram and paint the spare room pink, but nothing will quite prepare you for the drop. But when it happens you'll get resourceful and any good parent will make it work. You'll learn and grow through doing and it will add so much more to your life.

Decision is a mindset: Be a decision maker.

**Take action now.**

We're all lazy gits from time to time.

Come on, let's be honest here. All of us. There are so many things we just can't really be bothered to do. I [Rob] can't be bothered to cook. I never ever cook. Not even for girls. I hardly go shopping and I'm quite well known for it. I can't be bothered to do any cleaning and my Mum has to come over to water the plants otherwise they die. I'm 28, in case I didn't tell you.

I [Mark] can't really be bothered with all the trash that is on TV. There is much more to life that being infected by what I feel is not true to life. I can't be bothered with people who moan about their life and how rotten it is and never do anything about it. I know it sounds a little harsh, but in order to make things

Rob Moore & Mark Homer

work we all need to be proactive.

It is human nature to be lazy. The sad thing about it is that without actually doing anything about what you're reading here now, then there is no point in continuing.

Most people can't be bothered to make money, be wealthy and attract success, and would rather stay in their comfort zone of underachievement. It's much easier! We really hate to say it, but we know the statistics. Even if we try to pull some 'reverse psychology' on you and point out that *you will not* be one of those, 95% of you *will* be one of those! It's completely nuts.

Don't just read this to humour us or because you have heard about us, or maybe even because you like us; or because you don't. Read it for you. Make a decision right now that you are going to take action on what you are reading in this book.

Yes this is an obvious point, but really, so many people know what to do, or at least where to start, and they just don't do anything about it. Consistent action is the only way we are going to achieve wealth and success.

No one ever had a bag of money fall on their head whilst asleep, watching TV, meditating or playing the Playsation 2; at least not in our experience.

Pssst: if you can do that we bank at Barclays, our account

number is 50982756. Same day BACS works best for us!

It's all very well being great at visualisation and manifestation, and I strongly urge you to become masters in those Arts [we'll give you some help], but without doing anything about it, nothing will ever get done.

It really doesn't matter how fast or slow you take action, what direction you go in, or which strategy you use at first, as long as you continue to take action and you are open to opportunities [and growth].

## Summary

Be decisive, do a little more each day and always be moving forward. Use consistent action with never ending improvement and you will be as wealthy as you believe you can be. Procrastination is a disease. Now is always the best [and only] time.

Rob Moore & Mark Homer

# Section 3: The Secret Psychology of Successful Investors

Rob Moore & Mark Homer

Success, achievement or however you want to classify the life that you want leaves tracks and are all set up on basic concepts. Success is something that you can mould or mimic. Wealth is exactly the same. Once you know the mould or the strategy it then becomes predictable. Just like failure is predictable. As much as some may find it hard to believe that success is predictable; it really is. Anything is. Once you can find a pattern in something [a strategy] all you have to do is keep using that strategy over and over again to get your same, successful, predictable results. A mentor of ours used to tell us that you need your strategy to become so predictable that it gets boring. Then you know that it works.

Successful marketers do just that. Successful advertisers do just that. Tiger Woods does just that. How many times do you think he has practised [and visualised] the same shot?

You can take this one strategy and do just that; turn it into as much money as you want.

Those people who think that success is luck [we don't believe in luck: luck is a combination of knowledge, experience, opportunity] or co-incidence are most likely the people who are not where they want to be in their life. Now of course that does not relate to you. If we are to achieve anything then we need to start right here with ourselves.

If we want to change the world, it is generally our view of the world that needs to change. If we want to be in a position to be able to give back to others, something we really want to do here at Progressive Property, then we need to make sure that we have abundance and a good psychology for ourselves too. There is absolutely nothing selfish in building an asset base that can look after us, our families and our friends for generations to come. It's funny how so many people that we have met have had negative beliefs or guilt around making money. Again, not you, and as you are reading your strategies for becoming wealthy investing in Property will be becoming ever more clear now.

There are of course hundreds of things that we can look at in all kinds of detail, but this is not a life coaching manual. We have read a few though, and there are some very good ones out there, and as we see it at Progressive we can break down personal success, specific to Property investment profit, into the following categories…

# Know Your purpose

This is where everything is born. This is our reason for doing what we're doing and being who we are; why we are. This may seem like a big step, and it can take time [and believe me some say that it should], and that is just fine.

What are you investing for?

So many people are living their life in reaction to their mind and what they tell themselves; doing things they do not like [or love] and treading water on a day to day basis habitually. Perhaps they are working in a job that they hate with people that they hate.

It really doesn't have to be like that. Life is a **choice**. Everything is a choice. You don't have to set this in stone now but as you are formulating your strategy in your mind, also think about your purpose. Know why you are here.

Know what your purpose for making money is; what your purpose for investing in Property is. Is it to help your family? Is it to take care of the ones you love? Is it just to prove to yourself that you can do it? Is it to shut up all the negative people? Is it for a collection of super cars or matching shoes and handbags? Is it to spend on fast cars and fast women [and waste the rest]? Is it to leave a legacy or set up a foundation? Is it to grow a large business so that you can create many jobs? Is it so that you can be in a position to teach other people to do the same?

Rob Moore & Mark Homer

Whatever it is, you need to know it. Remember we have a section for you at the end of the book on page 371-375 where you can fill all of this in.

Money is just a consequence of the value we give to other people's lives. How can your purpose add to the lives of other people?

When you have a real purpose, when you are in your 'flow,' this will radiate and people will be attracted to your vision: to you [and many more properties will come your way too you know]. This is known as the 'why.' Once you have a compelling 'why' you will always find the 'how to.' In fact, the 'how to' becomes so easy.

If you have anything to add at the back of the book now, go to page 371-375 and write it down.

'Nothing is more powerful than a person who knows his destiny and has chosen *now* as the time to pursue it.' Jim Stovall.

## Summary

Know why you are here and for what purpose you are building your portfolio and your wealth. True purpose attracts success.

# Focus

You get what you focus on.

But chase too many rabbits & we end up catching none. Whatever it is that you think about most consistently is likely to become a reality in your life. We know that you know that. Top professional sportsmen are just that because they have focused on their sport and being the best for the greatest amount of time, with the greatest level of commitment.

Anyone who is an expert in their field is not so by accident, but because they have read the most books, done the most study, had the most learnings, made the most mistakes, and gained the most experience.

Thoughts become things.

Just think about flight. 500 years ago if you had told someone that anyone would be able to fly anywhere in the world in under a day you would probably have been voodoo'd, pinned to death and burned at the stake. Now it is common place because of people like the Wright brothers who believed that it could be done. They focused on making it happen, despite the fact that it had never been seen or done before.

If you want to be wealthy through your portfolio then you must think like the rich. The rich focus on wealth and money and business and success [without guilt]; learn how they think.

Rob Moore & Mark Homer

Find rich Property investors with 20 or more properties; people to mentor and coach you, and work out exactly what it is that they focus on the most. Where do they go, where do they work, eat and what people do they spend their time with the most? They are where they are because of their focus, and you can do and have exactly the same.

There will always be someone bigger, faster, richer, slimmer, prettier and more intelligent than us [but don't forget that it is all just perception or opinion]. However we all have unique qualities and we should focus on those rather than comparing what we have to others. If we all compared our wealth to that of Bill Gates then how happy would we allow ourselves to be?

Wherever you are is just where you should be, and in 1, 2 or 5 years from now you could quite easily have a Property portfolio that will look after you for the rest of your life, if you focus. Use the unique qualities that you have and become great at one thing.

Certainly the mistake that many of us make, and I have been guilty of this in the past [Rob again], is not focusing on one thing long enough to become so good at it that wealth and success are drawn to us.

In fact, let's go to page 374 and list them all now. It really doesn't matter what they are, and no one is watching; you might be surprised how many things you didn't think you were good at.

Ask yourself now what unique skills you have. Take a minute right now. What can you do that most people cannot? What are you better than most people at that you could become one of the best? You will be able to take many of these talents that you have focused on and turn them into cash in your portfolio.

Be opportunistic.

It is in focusing on something that we spot more opportunities. Have you ever noticed when you buy a new car that all of a sudden you see so many more of them on the road? Do you think that is because as soon as you buy your car everyone else copies you by buying the same car just to keep fashion with you, and then follows you around all day? Or perhaps it is because that car has now come into your awareness? And what about the terrible realisation that three girls are wearing the same dress as you at a party [especially if you are a man]?!

Focus works just like that. Be open minded and ever aware of the thousands of opportunities that are out there. Be thinking every minute of every day: 'How can I make the most of this situation.' Put a notebook by your bed and believe me you will wake up with ideas.

It's funny how things come to you with an even dose of focus and expectation.

Focus on a single Property type [the one that works the best for you in your area], focus on a single area, focus on your strategy

Rob Moore & Mark Homer

and refining it, focus on building relationships and offering value to people. Focus on your figures and you will be that financially independent Property investor that you can and want to be now.

At Progressive we have been refining a business model for a combined period of 5 years now. We have bought many properties of all types in that timeframe:

New build Property, off plan Property, overseas Property, cash-backs, houses of multiple occupancy [HMO], rent-backs; you name it, we have tried it. We have had the attitude that in order to gain the real knowledge and experience you need, you have to actually do it.

And yes we made some mistakes. Because we weren't focusing [we were trailblazing] on one strategy, we did not get the results that we were after. We bought too much too quickly in 2006, we did not have a specific set of rules so some properties were costing us more than we wanted per month. We tried some new build and overseas and found the yields to be very low, the rental figures and occupancy periods to be 'optimistic,' and so on and so on.

I [Mark] bought a flat in Bulgaria that ended up yielding a net of 1%. The amount of rent was grossly overvalued, the location was not quite as close to the ski lift as had been made out, and the thing never rented out for anywhere near as many weeks as

I was told per year. It was two years late and has caused me nothing but pain.

I've had the same problem with off plan properties, losing deposits in Florida and I've even had a respectable developer refuse to build a development after exchange! I'm sure you can't do that, but of course we have learned our lessons from these experiences. And what did happen was that we learned what worked and what doesn't, as we will explain later; where you will get the benefit of any mistakes we have made. In all of our experience in Property, and judging the performance of our own portfolio, focus is fundamental.

Try it if you don't believe us, we dare you!

We double dare you!

## Summary

Whatever it is that you want, focus on it intensely. Expect to achieve and you will. Stay on target in laser like fashion, don't chase too many rabbits and opportunities will come your way everyday.

Rob Moore & Mark Homer

# Belief

Wherever your ceiling of belief is now, that is the limit to what you believe you can achieve, you need to raise it. If you want more, then you need to **believe** you can achieve more.

If you want 5, 10 or 20+ properties then you need to believe you can have them now. That's right, before you own them. Some have found that tough, but if we were always waiting for evidence of something before we started, then obviously we would never achieve anything.

Did you know that if you catch fleas and put them in a jar they will jump to try and get out, only to hit the lid of the jar. If you leave them there for a while they will continue to do the same thing over and over: jumping and hitting the lid, expecting a different result [what was it Einstein said?]

Even more interesting is that when you take off the lid, the fleas will still only jump as high as where the jar lid was, even though they can jump higher and set themselves free. We are much more like fleas than we like to admit or realise, aren't we? Itch. Scratch.

Belief is the centre of everything, and it is our opinion (and we're not necessarily right) that we get what we believe we can achieve.

Rob Moore & Mark Homer

Our results are directly related to our level of belief. If we look at where we are now, the chances are we don't really believe that we can get a great deal more. Let us be honest with ourselves here, if we did, we would have more and be more, wouldn't we?

That has to change. Think about what having 20 properties would feel and look like to you. Think about 50. Think about the lifestyle that it will bring you now...

Go on; actually think about it right now [the Law of attraction]...

And while you are allow me to tell you a little story about the Law of attraction [Rob]. Take this as you will to the level at which you believe it. In 2004/5, when I realised that I had been living like a bit of an idiot for 25 years and a friend of mine just happened to give me two sets of Tony Robbins tapes [attraction?], something very exciting occurred for me.

I had been learning about visualisation, incantations and repeating things to yourself so much that 1. You actually believe it [like being 'rich' before you are rich] and 2. You are far more likely to attract it through awareness and focus that I thought to myself; what have I got to lose?

So I tried it.

I used to get up at 6:30 every morning for 99 days [that's how long it took] and get on my exercise bike in my front room and look out of my window onto my driveway.

'Every day in every way I'm getting bigger and better and stronger yes! I'm wealthy, successful and I have a Nissan 350Z with orange leather seats sitting on my drive.'

At the time of starting I had £30,000 worth of debt and no job:

'Every day in every way I'm getting bigger and better and stronger yes! I'm wealthy, successful and I have a Nissan 350Z with orange leather seats sitting on my drive.'

And there was no proof that any of this stuff actually worked because I it was a whole new world to me:

'Every day in every way I'm getting bigger and better and stronger yes! I'm wealthy, successful and I have a Nissan 350Z with orange leather seats sitting on my drive.'

99 days later I had my gunmetal 350Z [by far my favourite car at the time, regardless of price, and the sexiest thing on 4 wheels] sitting on my drive with orange leather seats [I didn't even know that they made them with orange leather seats!]. It was mine, I owned it, and I loved it. Of course this is just my experience and it doesn't mean that you can or will do the same now.

The difference between the amount of money you or I make and what Bill Gates makes is down to belief. Now we are not saying you can go out now and make serious amounts of money...

And what we **are** saying is that by following all the strategies in this book and applying them with a heightened belief that you will achieve whatever you desire now; your results **will** change accordingly.

When we started in Property everyone was telling us it was too late. When we were buying with no money everyone was telling us it couldn't be done. When we gave up high paying jobs people thought we were nuts. When we set up Progressive to help other people do the same we were told we shouldn't:

"There aren't enough properties"

"People won't pay you to help them"

"You're too young; I've been doing it 30 years"

We refused to listen [crabs and sheep] and be held back. We used it to motivate us, and it gave us a burning desire to succeed and to prove them wrong. No one will ever tell us we can't do anything.

We have never looked back.

You have to trust us on this one. Well actually you don't; it is your choice. If you do choose to trust us now, don't be like most people and wait to see results before you start to believe that you can have what you want. You could be waiting a very long time.

## Summary

Believe *now* that you can achieve what you want to achieve and see the results change accordingly. Believe in yourself. Don't listen to the crabs. Add commitment and hard work to that belief and you have the keys to great success in your portfolio and your life.

# Anyone can do it

## And yes that includes You

You are your biggest chance of success and your biggest chance of failure. If you don't believe that you can have the wealth and Property investment success that you want, then you won't. It is that simple. Having just read about belief, let's assume that you believe [or are working on the belief] that you can achieve any goal you put your mind to.

It doesn't matter if you don't have all the answers right now: none of us have all the answers. This book will give you a big leap forward, but the rest of your success will be down to your own belief and consistent action.

Remember that we used the analogy that buying a Property is like having your first child. Ok, to all the mothers out there, we are by no means saying that we could even begin to understand the pain you went through. But at the end of the day when it happens for the first time we're all in the same boat; we all start from the same place and we all have it in us to be good parents; even though we might not know it yet!

And it's amazing how resourceful we become when we're actually doing it; when we're in at the deep end.

You know that anyone can do it. Think about it. You know that most entrepreneurs, multi-millionaire businessmen and Property

Rob Moore & Mark Homer

investors started from somewhere. Very often that somewhere is much further back than where you are right now. I [Rob] was £30,000 in debt when I started.

Just look at anything you have achieved in the past: anything at all.

Come on, let's do it now. Everyone has unique talents and we know that you are good at something; many things in fact. Whatever it is that you are thinking now that you are good at, where you have achieved levels of success, you can replicate. Napoleon Hill calls it transmutation. Think of all that wayward sexual energy a lot of us have [speak for ourselves?!] and the huge amount of energy people expend [waste] on negative things that serve them no purpose. Imagine if we could hone that in and use that energy in attaining wealth and success. We'd all be multi-squillionaires!

Our guess is you got really good at something through focus, belief, confidence, hard work, teamwork, commitment and concentration, to name just a few. We shall be talking about these later.

There is enough money out there for us all to be millionaires many many times over. There are enough properties out there for everyone who reads this book to have a nice profitable portfolio.

Money does not choose where it goes and does not

discriminate. There is no one single 'type' of person that becomes wealthy. Regardless of age, race, upbringing, creed, nurture and health, we can all become wealthy right now.

If you believe you can be wealthy, with an effective Property strategy to boot, you will attract wealth. Anyone can do it, especially you.

## Take personal responsibility now

Do you know anybody who is always blaming other people for things that go wrong? Perhaps even your boss or partner? Maybe you know people who always blame the weather or bad luck for their misfortunes. People who say 'it only ever happens to me:' people who are never wrong and nothing is ever their fault.

I remember [Rob], being a competitive golfer in my youth, consistently blaming the wind for my poor scores. The irony is that the same wind blows on us all, doesn't it?

If only I knew then what I know now. If, but, when, maybe, shoulda, woulda, coulda: whatever!

Of course this is not you, but there are many people out there who have this attitude. That is their decision to be like that, and of course we have no problem with it at all.

However this is not the attitude of wealthy and successful Property investors. The most wealthy and successful people, investors and business owners understand **responsibility**. The performance of their assets is not due to market movements, but their own diligence, faith, persistence and following of the 'rules' as discussed in this book.

We know that for the long term our attitudes and decisions will serve us well if they are positive and follow the rules in this section.

The very best mentors that we have studied will take no responsibility for success; they will lay all the plaudits to the members of their team. However when things go wrong or challenges arise they will be the first to throw up their hands and take full responsibility for the situation. Then change it.

Don't blame the market or the estate agent or the vendor. Your effective strategy and desire to continually improve will be your key to Property wealth and success.

The more we take responsibility for everything that happens in our life, everything that we have control over, every decision we make, the more we will be in control of the things that happen in our life.

Are you fully in control? If not do not worry [or blame someone else!] just read on with an open mind now.

Take responsibility for your life, your decisions and your finances now.

## Money is not the answer, you are

If you think that money is the answer to all of your life problems, then your problems are only just starting.

Money is not the answer.

Many of our business mentors state that with more money bigger problems come. Of course a problem is a perception, and the wealthiest see these so called 'problems' as challenges or opportunities. It is vital for us to realise that money doesn't solve anything.

Take a look at your money beliefs again:

"Money is one of the most important subjects of your entire life. Some of life's greatest enjoyments and most of life's greatest disappointments stem from your decisions about money. Whether you experience great peace of mind or constant anxiety will depend on getting your finances under control." Robert Allen.

We regularly check ours to see that they are where we want them to be, and to make sure they work for us at Progressive [and in our personal lives].

Money is easy to attract because you have the unique abilities to attract it. Money is not prejudiced and you can have whatever belief, religion or political standpoint you choose, and still be wealthy.

You are the answer.

We must remember that money and happiness are completely unrelated. Some of the happiest people are the poorest and some of the most horrible revolting nasty people are wealthy beyond imagination. It probably won't last, but there we go. Don't look to money for the answers. You can choose to be whoever you want, regardless of how much wealth you have now and how much more you will make in the future.
You are the answer.

Your portfolio is your vehicle to do the things you want in your life, but it does not depend on it. Wealth is merely a consequence of whatever it is that you do. The harder and faster and smarter you work, the more money you will attract, but it is still just a result of that.

Those who continually spend more than they earn [even when they earn a great deal] are chasing their tails in a self fulfilling vicious circle: always chasing more money to be happier only to spend more than they earn and feel empty. We personally know of someone who earns a nice salary of £200,000 per year and is so heavily in debt.

Money doesn't judge. Money doesn't think: 'She's got long legs; I'm going to hang around with her.' Money doesn't think: 'He's got an I.Q of 266; I'm going to stick with him.' Money really doesn't think.

Money is drawn to those who attract it: those who learn how to attract it and those who want it the most. Those who make the right decisions to get it and take consistent action to find and keep it, have it. And lots of it.

**Have everything now**

Remember that money is not the answer? Well if you have forgotten already we have some work to do together, don't we?!

You have everything you need *right now* to be as wealthy as you want to be; as wealthy as you believe that you want to be.

With the help of this book we would like to think that you have the tools and guidance that you need. You know this already, don't you? Let's face it, we're not changing the world or telling you anything new here. We know that you can make the choices you need to make, and that you have everything you need, now.

We all do.

Rob Moore & Mark Homer

You can choose exactly what you want now. You can have wealth and happiness and free time and a social life and a great family life and time with your kids and partner who you love dearly and who feels appreciated and holidays 3 times a year and regular sex and breakfast in bed [or both at once]...

You really can have it all, and it is only belief that will ever tell us otherwise.

## Summary

Anyone can do it; especially you. Believe that you can and you will and know that you have the answers you need. Take personal responsibility for your life, your decisions and your finances and have what you want for your life.

# Faith, passion and desire

Can you think of anyone who really loves what they do?

**Passion**: people who have passion and desire in what they do are radiant, attractive and successful in their own right and by their own definition. Think of Tony Robbins or Mother Teresa or Mohammad Ali. Passion for what we do and a desire to make it work is absolutely essential for our own personal success and happiness.

It is essential for our portfolio wealth.

Have passion and desire in everything you do and faith that it will work for you, otherwise don't waste your time doing it; passion and desire really will make a huge difference. Remember everything is our *choice*. Be passionate and desire the best for yourself.

We love Property. Property is King. Property is our God. We live and breathe Property because it makes us so much money. Property is our passion, vocation and guardian angel. We turned our desire to become financially independent into passion and then everything changed; everything started to happen [and didn't stop]. If you have read Christopher Howard's book: 'Turning passion into profits,' then you will know exactly where we are coming from.

**Faith**: Faith in ourselves [or a higher entity that we may believe in] is another essential ingredient to personal and Property investment success. If we do not implicitly trust ourselves or believe in who we are, what we're doing and that we *will* get where we want to be, then who is going to?

It sounds so easy in practice, and the truth is that it is, especially with a nice dose of passion and desire.

Have we told you the Colonel Sanders story? For those of you who don't know it, and those that want to hear it again, Colonel Sanders was over 65 before he even got the KFC brand off the ground. He spent 2 years travelling across America, sleeping in his car, taking his special recipe from restaurant to restaurant in the hope [belief] that someone would like it. Do you think he had faith in himself and his recipe? You know the rest of the story.

## Summary

Have faith in yourself and whatever you believe in; that you are and will become great at making profit through Property. Be passionate and have a burning desire for success and you will get it.

# Be realistic

Set your expectations, be realistic and take your time.

This was something that I found so hard in the beginning [Rob]. I was so focused and excited and determined and energetic and impatient that I wanted everything yesterday and made these huge goals and felt amazing. They were unrealistic.

Goals, dreams and vision are all essential parts of seeing your future before it happens and making plans to get there. Some of the greatest business people are those who can vividly picture their life in its future exactly how it looks: exactly how it will be. Richard Branson is great at this.

Can you picture your life in 1 year? 2 years? 5 years from now?

And with this ability, it is just as essential to understand what we need to do on a daily basis, and how we are going to realistically achieve what we want to achieve. Being overly dreamy or unrealistic about the market, about goals and projections and fact is dangerous, and will damage your long term wealth and security.

There are times when we need to keep our feet on the ground. We always need to take consistent action to get to where we want to be; things are not going to always go our way, and we will make mistakes. What are our expectations of these? How will we deal with situations when life throws us a curveball? It is always very wise to be realistic.

Perhaps, at this stage, you may be thinking 'these guys are contradicting themselves a little.' They talk about visualisation and big goals, yet they talk about being 'grounded' and 'realistic.'

Life is all about opposites.

Just ponder that for a second. You know this already. We can't have black without white, love without its polar opposite. Life, as well as Property investment, is about balance and equilibrium.

Imagine just having the capacity to dream without ever achieving anything; life would be one big tease; you can look but you can't touch!

Then think about losing your ability to dream. Don't imagine it, because you can't. Don't picture everything in your life that you want; because you can't...

This is one of the reasons that we feel fortunate [not lucky] and why we think our partnership has achieved what it has; and will continue to do so indefinitely. Your authors are very different people. You may have noticed some of these differences already. Mark needs evidence; Rob doesn't always need to know how everything works. Mark has to do all the figures 10 times over, Rob is happy to go with his intuition. Mark likes working with people, Rob is happy to lock himself away for a week and bury himself in the computer if it needs to be done. Mark buys a car for the 0-60 times, bhp, mpg, torque figures and residual value Rob buys it because it looks bad ass. Mark buys a shirt because it fits well, is tailored with darts and has a 15" collar with Oxford weave, Rob buys one because it is a peacock!

A big part of being realistic is to watch and study what other successful people have achieved. Sam Walton of Wall Mart was an expert at watching his competition and taking on the things that worked well. If someone who has been in the industry takes 5 years to build 50 properties is it realistic to try to buy 100 in your first year?

Look at history. Look at what others have done and in what timescale they have achieved their successes. Know the 'ifs and buts' [without focusing on them too much], and set your expectation at the right place from the start.

Remember that success is as much a mindset as it is a destination or outcome.

Never stretch yourself too far. Do not invest money that you absolutely cannot live without and always have a contingency. We recommend that in every £100,000 that you set aside for investment, £70,000 should be invested and £30,000 should be set aside as contingency. This is vital and will be discussed later.

## Summary

Be realistic and set your expectations at the right level from the start. Never stretch yourself too far and always have contingencies in place for worst case scenarios.

# Think mid-long term

Long term sustainability.

Rome wasn't built in a day. Nor were all of the wealthy Property investors. If we want to get wealthy, be wealthy and stay wealthy, then we need to think long term sustainability rather than immediate gratification.

Building a portfolio takes time, regardless of what you might be told. Money attracts money and compounds [both ways]. If we keep spending all we earn then we'll never have long term wealth, because we're not saving/investing long enough to attract more of it.

Property is exactly the same. If we keep selling them instead of holding to build a portfolio, then we will never be in a position to compound earnings and become very wealthy for the long term.

Does this make sense? We've got more on this one for you later on.

In formulating your Property strategy think about this: will any decision aid my long term wealth? Is this sustainable? Will this create a good return on investment [ROI]? If not then leave and move on.

The principles set about in this book all gear towards long term wealth and sustainability, because that is the only way. If the product, investment or decision doesn't fall within your set parameters then walk on by and let someone else take the gamble.

Whatever you do be careful of 'get rich quick zero to a million in no time' type offers, ads and 'opportunities.' We love the way most of them are sold: 'I have this great opportunity for you!' Oh yeah? What is it? Well I can't tell you now but what I can tell you...

Yes Ok. No thank you. If it seems far too good to be true then the chances are that it is. By all means be open minded, but do your diligence. Every day we get approached by so many of these companies and when we do our diligence we have always found that the *actual* results are never the same.

Let me tell you this based on our personal experience: most people [not all] in network marketing companies are not making any money, despite what they might tell you. Most 'home based business opportunities' need about 60 hours a week for very little money. Think of all those Ponzi/Pyramid schemes that promised the earth and robbed people of their money.

Most self-professed Property squillionaires are paying thousands upon thousands every year just to stay afloat. Warren Buffett looks for stocks that have longevity and sustainability, and you should be doing the same for your education, career, business and investments.

Think 1, 2, 5 and 10 years ahead and think about your future and your goals. Will your decisions to invest put you nearer or further away from these? Will that car, that conservatory or that 3 week holiday to Magaluf add to your long term wealth?

In five years you can have as many material things and 'liabilities' as you want. If it's a Ferrari you truly desire, and you love the thought of driving in the summer evenings with the roof down and the music on full, then make sure you can afford it ten times over so that you can actually enjoy it without worrying about the cost of the petrol and servicing.

If you want an 8 bed mansion with stables and a heart shaped bed with a Leopard skin throw then make sure you work up to it; enjoy the journey without worrying about what the heating bills will be for the next quarter. Build your portfolio and wealth steadily and over time on solid financial and educational foundations.

If you can't be bothered with all of this then burn this book and try to sue a big company or marry a King or Princess, but remember that everything comes at a price; and that might just be your happiness.

## Summary

Think long term. Will any investment decision aid your sustainable success? If something seems too good to be true then it probably is, so walk on by and leave the gambling to the gamblers. Stick to your strategy and be forever wealthy for generations to come.

# Trust Your instincts

## Instinct and intuition

Your instincts and your intuition have been with you since the day you were born. They are part of you and who you are and have grown with you.

Everything that you have ever learned or experienced has been 'stored' in your subconscious. You have an innate ability to 'thin slice' any situation. Have you read 'Blink' by Malcolm Gladwell? This is a great book on this subject. Go to

www.progressiveproperty.co.uk/readinglist.asp

if you want to get yourself a copy now.

You can process millions of pieces of information in milli-seconds and make shrewd judgements that you may not have made so well had you stopped to think about it. This is your instinct and intuition at work. It is there to protect you and to help you. Trust it. Trust yourself and what your subconscious tells you.

If you get a bad feeling about something absolutely don't go through with it. Do not work with or buy from someone you don't like, you don't trust, or who gives you an 'odd' feeling. There is a very good chance that your subconscious is telling you something. Trust it.

Rob Moore & Mark Homer

We can all get excited when an apparently amazing deal or offer is presented to us. Sometimes good [excited] feelings can lead us into problems because we are avoiding any due diligence. If you get a good feeling then by all means do the research to back up your feeling and pat yourself on the back if you are right.

If you get a bad feeling then run like the bloody wind!

Stick to this strategy and you will not go wrong. The odd chance might pass you by but all in all you will be right to listen to yourself. It is all about trusting yourself to trust yourself!

There are so many great, honest, skilled and trusted people out there. There is just no need to risk your wealth and future by working with people who are anything less than right for you.

Trust is everything in life, in business, in wealth, in relationships, with other people; in absolutely everything. It can take a lifetime to build a team of trusted people, when you find them hold on to them for dear life.

Let's face it, you know when something is wrong, and you know you know, even if you try your hardest to tell yourself otherwise. We've all been in relationships we knew weren't right, haven't we? Life is far too short, in our opinion, to waste our time.

Trust yourself. Believe in your ability to make the right unconscious decisions now.

And if you are sitting here demanding evidence for all of this then create a strategy around it and stick to it:

1. Listen to what you tell yourself
2. Do your diligence. Find fact and respected opinion on your gut feeling
3. Make an informed decision as to whether you will act on your instinct or not, and get advice from those who have trodden the path
4. Act fast or move on

## Summary

Don't get lured in by people or things that don't feel right; you just don't need to. Trust your instincts and intuition and live with your informed decisions; they will end up being right.

Rob Moore & Mark Homer

# Expect the unexpected

## Contingency

Planning and preparation are absolutely essential in Property wealth and success. There are very few people who had lasting wealth or a 20 + Property portfolio by total accident. Although it may appear that way on the surface, the fact is that wealthy people who are self made are great planners.

They may appear 'lucky.' In our experience, that is what envious or unsuccessful people say of those that have done well. If we take the time to look closely and to ask the right questions, we soon learn that there are principles that successful and wealthy people follow that anyone can follow.

**Fundamental tip No.5:
The only difference between those that are wealthy and those that are not is **consciousness**.

Wealthy and successful people do things 'unconsciously' that others are not even conscious of yet. They have done this through habit or repetition, experience or knowledge. Anyone can do this, anyone can get the experience or knowledge required to make these 'secrets' [what most people don't know that successful people do] become automatic and 'unconscious.'

Do your diligence as explained previously. **Always** do your diligence. It will become second nature, but for the mean time you will have to just drum it in. Know the worst case scenario, so that no matter what happens nothing comes as too much of a surprise that it knocks you on your knees. Be prepared for many situations that could arise and not just the one that you expect [or desire].

Know how much you want to save and never touch. Know how much you want to invest and don't push it too far. Have a separate account for unexpected costs [that absolutely will come up; especially if you have not opened this account]. Know how much tax free cash you can save on an annual basis. Know how much you can afford to risk. Know the difference between investing and gambling and understand risk assessment.

Know what other people want. Find out what they need. Know that people have their own agenda to any deal and make sure that you are aware of it so that a) you can strike the best deal, b) you can strike the best win-win relationship and c) you don't get ripped off.

Always check the small print on any contract or agreement. Check the interest rates, charges and fees of everything [especially when borrowing] and don't be afraid to negotiate and shop around as you can always find a better deal. Do not believe the first figure that you are told, and do not settle for a deal you are not happy with.

Good people to listen to are the wealthy, the very successful, investors with a portfolio of 10 or more properties, the ones who have the skills and knowledge that you require, and the ones who are already doing it.

People you shouldn't listen to can very often be the closest to you, and this can be hard for some people. Friends and family may have [or think they have] the best intentions, but they can very often hold you back without even knowing that they are doing it. Are they experts in Property?

You shouldn't listen to people who have zero experience, who aren't clearly doing it themselves, who think they know everything about everything, conspiracy theorists and people who are drunk or on narcotics.

**Grow and accept change**

If living things are not growing, they're dying. In this world, there is actually no such thing as standing still. It is forwards or backwards. Stagnation/lack of movement means you are actually falling behind.

Growth, evolution of the self and the acceptance that things don't stay the same are so important in your mindset and achievement of wealth and success.

Look at the internet. 20 years ago there was barely such a thing. Now you can do and find absolutely anything on the internet. Believe me, anything. Had you speculated about the evolution of the technological age 20 years ago, not even the most skilled forecasters could have predicted such phenomenal movement in technology.

And the sad and unfortunate thing for many is that those who do not stay up to date with the fast moving world get left behind. They stagnate. They die.

Many people have lived a life a certain way for such a long time and are so resistant to change. It is so counter productive and such a waste of energy trying to fight the trends of change. Imagine trying to use an abacus for Pythagoras or going shopping with half pennies!

One thing that inspires us is youth. Youth is our position of strategic advantage in this game. All of our perceptions of youth are different, but those who have a young and fresh mind can very often lack fear and be very flexible. Being flexible is very important nowadays, more than ever, and it's only going to become more important. Those who are not flexible will get left behind.

Your wealth and portfolio success depends on growth. This is not just accepting the things that are new, but growing within ourselves. All the things that you are learning here, all of which you already know now, will help your growth and evolution, and your attainment of your life of choice.

Buy to Let did not exist until the mid 90's, and then Property investment changed. It is changing all the time and now more and more houses are getting rented out room by room. It will continue to change, believe us it will.

Your needs *will* change over time too. A lot will depend on your age, education and your emotional mood. The people you know and deal with will change. Society will change. The rates from the bank and the value of money will change. The way you spend 'money' and what you want it for will change. The mortgage products will change and the economy will change. Understand this very important concept and *accept* it. Revise your strategy as you feel the need and know that you are on your path, and that growth and change are part of your journey.

## Summary

Plan, prepare and be ready for the unexpected. Know that the market and your strategy will evolve and change over time. Don't resist it; accept it. Be flexible, versatile and decisive.

# Delay gratification

## Discipline

Discipline is the ability to control yourself and your desires/urges for instant gratification. It is the ability to stick to your strategy, and not be lured or tempted by anything that glistens or is coated in chocolate.

We have regularly talked about buying a Ferrari each. Sometimes we think: screw it. We are young. We have a nice portfolio; let's remortgage a couple and enjoy ourselves. He who dares, wins, Rodney!

And then we did the figures. A brand new Ferrari 430 will cost [taking everything into account: loan repayments, depreciation, servicing, maintenance] £40,000 in the first year to own. That's **£40,000**. That is about 4 year's growth on 4 little properties. You need a salary of £70,000 just to pay for your car [before you can eat].

Most people who get to a salary of £50,000 think they can buy these kinds of toys. They can't [unless they want to be in serious debt for the rest of their life]. You need a salary of at least £200,000 to fund a Ferrari.

Remember we said that wealth is a mindset. Wealth is the ability to attract money, success, value and happiness, and not just the amount of money you have in the bank.

Rob Moore & Mark Homer

Do not be lured by cash-backs and inflated prices/huge apparent new build discounts. By the end of this book you will have many ideas for a simple, clear, effective and proven strategy.

When you go out into the world to apply the things you are reading here, there will be offers and people and e-mails and all sorts thrown at you left right and centre about how you can be a millionaire in 10 minutes.

Be disciplined.

Remember the rules for success and stick to your strategy that should be becoming more and more clear as you read.

Let your investments grow. Do not eat away at them too early. Set up solid foundations by understanding this principle. In the mid-long term you will be far wealthier with a significant portfolio than those who over borrowed, spent too much too soon, didn't do their diligence and were allured by the dark side!

## Summary

Be disciplined!

# Never give up

### Persistence

As Winston Churchill famously said (and repeated): never ever ever give up!

Endearing persistence (not cat-like annoyance) is absolutely essential in your quest for personal success. We have great friends who have persisted when to the outside world it has looked like the chances of success were negligible; in many areas of life such as relationships, health and wealth.

It took Thomas Edison ten thousand experiments to finally see the light in his invention of the light bulb. He did not give up, and knew that with every 'failure' he was one step closer to his goal. Failure is only an option when we give up, until then we are still moving forward.

There were many times when we could have given up; times when the deals we bought weren't the best we could have bought; times when we had nasty surveyors down value perfectly good Property; times when, as directors of a previous Property company, we were generating all of the sales for a very small share of the reward.

Our story of persistence is, to be honest, not as glorious as some. For some great stories you need to read 'Think and Grow Rich' by Napoleon Hill.

Rob Moore & Mark Homer

www.progressiveproperty.co.uk/readinglist.asp

We would love to tell you that we had 3 near death experiences [I only had 2 – Rob!] and jumped through rings of fire, but most people's lives aren't really like that. Yes we got into debt at some points and it was hard. I [Rob] had to borrow money off just about everyone I knew to get me to a position of comfort, and yes the market changed a few times and gave us a few eye opening surprises, but there really is no secret formula here other than **attrition**. Just keep going, you only fail when you stop; so just don't stop. Be the Duracell bunny.

The sad thing about this is that so many people actually get quite close to any desired goal. They get most of the hard lessons they need to toughen them up for the future, and then give up.

Everything we do gets to a tipping point, where all the hard work we put in, [like getting the knowledge to go out and get great discounts or building a solid and reliable contact base] will pay dividends. Once those foundations are set then the money starts to roll your way; but not before.

Take this book, for example. "The 44 Most Closely Guarded Property Secrets" has taken around 2390 days and close to 12,000 hours to get from the ether to your hands. Now there are many people who are taking this information and turning it into cash. You have probably read many of our testimonials showing what can be done if we stick at it and break through that 'tipping point.'

Take Neil Asher, for example. Neil has one of the most successful global Life Coaching companies in the world, New Insights. I wouldn't be right to tell you in our words what he achieved, so this short passage is from an email he sent us as soon as he had read this book:

"As a direct result of one of the many secrets in the book, I purchased a property in Brighton for 12% BMV & have made £27,000 in 3 months, all whilst having a baby daughter!

Rob & Mark actually do what they teach rather than the so called 'Guru's who talk the talk but still work in Sainsbury's at the weekend. If you have any interest whatsoever in setting yourself financially free you have to read this book now!"

You can take that one step further and "Make Cash in a Property Market Crash"

www.progressiveproperty.co.uk/book2-buy-now.asp

Don't be one of those people who nearly got there, have great stories of how they nearly made it, or could have been if but when and maybe. Own yourself, not your story.

Rob Moore & Mark Homer

## Summary

Never giving up and having faith in ourselves will send us on our desired path and get us where we want to be. The education we get in the process is absolutely vital in our growth. Just don't ever ever give up. Ever.

What you have been given here are the tools to have the mindset of the wealthy and successful. Yes this applies to Property, but it is not exclusive to just bricks and mortar, it should carry through the whole of your life.

I [Rob] have to admit that it took me 25 years to get this. It took me that long to understand that I was responsible for my own life and results and that there are things that can be learned that will make you rich, happy and successful. I really did think it was genetic; down to where I lived and who had the most luck. I thought that it was everybody else who was lucky [Remember luck is a combination of knowledge, experience and opportunity].

I now know that to be a complete fallacy. It's nonsense. It's utter rubbish. We can be all that we want to be. You can be all that you want to be. I know because I have done it for myself and I have coached so many people and helped them do the same. When it comes down to it, we're all made of the same stuff.

Think 'How can I do it?' rather than 'I can't do it,' believe that anything can be achieved, seek to learn new things and take consistent decisive action everyday, and you are there.

Rob Moore & Mark Homer

# Section 4: Secret Tips to Profit, Beat the Best & Retire Rich & Happy

This is where it all starts to get interesting. You now have your blue belt. Well done! Most don't get this far. You know the basics and the principles and you can go out there and look after yourself on the street.

Mastery comes when you step it up a gear and things happen naturally: subconsciously. The following concepts, rules, Laws, secrets; call them what you will, will be the difference that makes the difference. They will be the things that set you apart from those that do not do [the lazy ones].

This will exponentially improve your money making ability. These are some of the things that we have spent many years refining. To be exact; over £650,000 has been invested in properties and education to bring you the lessons we teach you in this book. 4 failed relationships and 5 properties that lost us money have been endured because of our passion for Property and our commitment to investment.

Perhaps some of it might sound obvious: good! You know that your strategy is developing nicely.

Onward...

Rob Moore & Mark Homer

# Understand the language of Property

If you wanted to get by in France [just a random example]: live, eat, shop, socialise, learn, have a loving relationship, do you think you would be able to if you could not speak a word of French [and did not have a translator for all you smart asses?!] You would probably find it very difficult. You would need to spend time learning the language, wouldn't you?

So why is it that most people who want to be rich are not financially literate? Why is it that many Property investors do not understand the language of Property investing and the language of money?

If you want to be wealthy, then you need to be able to speak the language of money. If you want your wealth in Property, then you need to be able to speak the language of Property.

Language is the gateway to our thoughts. It is the medium in which we communicate and we understand. Our continual study of the language of Property will be directly proportional to the amount of money we earn, [unless you get someone you trust to do it for you].

Do you understand BTL, LTV, BMV, DIP, HMO, RICS, ROI, COC, ROCE? [Isn't it annoying when people use too many acronyms?]. Do you understand the difference between gross yield and net yield? [It seems that most Property clubs and companies don't]. How about colloquial phrases such as upside

Rob Moore & Mark Homer

down, underwater, prop, val, reval, repo, refurb, redec, shortfall?

Ok enough. Don't worry; we're going to help you out here. For a jargon busting list you can log on to our website at

www.progressiveproperty.co.uk/jargondictionary.asp

It is just a basic jargon buster but of course the more you read and the more you do, and the better you get, the more you will understand, and the more money you will make.

What books and publications do you read and what websites do you use? What is your homepage? Who do you spend the most time with? It will all have a bearing on how quickly you pick up the language.

Language is such an underrated tool. This was an absolute epiphany for us when we learned this, and so ridiculously simple to implement. Our words are, as already stated, the gateway to everything we do and the nearest thing to articulating our thoughts. The language that we use is a direct representation of the knowledge we have of a subject.

# Summary

Improve your Property and financial language. The language you use is a representation of your thoughts and your knowledge. Improve your knowledge on the subjects of Property and money and your results will be proportionate. Your Property wealth will skyrocket.

# Be a relationship expert

## You are Your Wealth

In this chapter, we're going to talk about 'artistry.'

This is your licence to have fun. This is all about getting your desired outcomes; getting what you want in a way that helps and empowers others.

Though more holistic than just Property, this is likely where you will either succeed or fail: where you will be the 1 out of the 100 that did or 1 of the 99 that tells the stories of why they didn't, wouldn't, shouldn't and couldn't.

Before we even start investing, and having read section 3, we know that our success starts with ourselves.

It has little to do with any outside factors such as the market or other people being unreliable and selfish. As long as we keep going and as long as we learn from the mistakes we make along the way, then we will get to that 5, 10 or 50 strong portfolio, or whatever it is that we want to be, do and have.

One of the biggest factors in our success will come down to the relationships we build, the contact base we have, the team we have around us working in harmony, and ultimately the way we treat other people.

Rob Moore & Mark Homer

There are many people out there with what seems like big businesses treating people badly and using them, and believe us because we have met many of them; you would not want to live their lives.

Every good relationship you build could be the key to setting up a deal that will make you money, no matter how insignificant or removed it may actually seem. Someone always knows someone who knows someone who could be the link that you need.

The person right in front of you may not necessarily have an immediate answer that you need now, but she may have in 6 months, or someone she knows may have, or someone she knows. Long term thinking is especially important in relationship building.

Always be fair and honest with people and think about what you can offer them and the value that you can add to their lives; they will always want to help you in return.

**Fundamental tip No.6:
If you help enough people get what they want, you'll get what you want.

We hope that you will agree that at Progressive we give away a lot of very valuable information for free. In fact, this book may have been the first time that you have actually paid [and we don't get much of that £20] to gain any Property knowledge from us, having perhaps read our eBooks, eCourses, attended our tele-seminars and open days; none of which would have cost you any money.

This is the way we like to do business. We don't have to hide what we know; we should all be sharing it. Interestingly our statistics actually prove that more of you will invest with us now because we have been open with our information and given value. This is despite the fact that we are actually teaching you to do what we do and that in the long run you don't even need us. Interesting isn't it?

We aren't just talking about brokers, financiers, vendors [discussed more in detail in this section], agents, solicitors, designers, printers, clients, staff and business associates for your relationship expertise; we are talking about everyone you meet.

There are some key skills that will get you a very long way in building a very large and profitable Property portfolio, and of course in life in general.

### Importance:

Perhaps the most effective skill in being a relationship expert is understanding people's inherent and basic need to feel important and significant. We all have it, it's one of the 6 basic human needs hardwired into our neurology.

It is the job of a relationship and Property expert to find out an individual's trigger for feeling important and using it. It makes people feel great, and when they feel great they'll help you, like you and go out of their way for you. It will make you feel great too!

If you're not convinced, piss them off and see how they help you then!

In our experience some of the most common ways to make people feel important are compliments of success, power, proactivity, friendship, attention and listening, admiration, things they're good at or skills [with the opposite sex is a big one! Tell someone they're a stud and watch them puff their chest out!], their taste and choices and so on.

In our opinion it's best to mean what you say and be honest. Don't be a sycophant [ass-kisser], be genuine, find one thing you really like and mention it.

We do it to each other all the time and we don't even know it. If I want to make Rob feel good all I have to do is mention something good about Progressive's marketing or his cowboy boots or that his arms are looking bigger and I can see him light up!

And to make Mark feel important I know I can comment on his buying skills, his driving skills or how comprehensive and detailed his latest spreadsheet is!

*Listening:*

People talk too much; much too much. If we spent more time listening we'd actually find the answers that are staring us in the face!

No-one really cares about our crappy day or boring mundane Groundhog Day life. People just want to tell you above theirs! Funnily enough, many people get importance and significance from this.

Great listeners build quick rapport, make people feel important and get the answers they need. A good rule of thumb for any conversation is to speak for one third and listen for two thirds. This is so important it almost made our 'Fundamental tips.' Try it and see. You might just be surprised.

*Asking questions:*

This has quite a lot in common with listening. A great way to get people to talk for two thirds of the conversation is to ask questions. It is amazing how simple this one is, yet most people we talk to are...

incessantabouttalkingaboutthemselveswithouttakingabreath.

The more questions we ask, the more answers we get. The better questions we ask, the better answers we get.

The best leaders and relationship experts get the most out of the people around them. They treat them like family and ultimately become very successful. Be sure to treat everyone fairly, equally and with their viewpoint in mind, and you are most of the way to becoming a relationship expert. Then [and only then] can you go out and make a shed load of money in Property!

To structure a Property deal takes many people, far more than in many other areas of investment. Your ability to empower people will determine your results.

And it is actually quite easy. Put yourself in the other person's shoes and don't be a shark [as there are many out there] and there you have it: the magic secret formula.
Genius eh?!

## Summary

Treat everyone well and with respect. Think about how you can add value to their lives and become a relationship expert. Everyone you meet could be the missing link you need for success and profit.

## Choose Your investment area carefully

This is one of the most misunderstood concepts in the Property world. Seriously, there are so many people and companies out there investing all over the place: villas in Spain, ski flats in Bulgaria, second homes in Cyprus, and properties dotted all over the UK.

And why do they do this?

"I want a diverse portfolio."

"It is good to spread your risk."

Well Warren Buffet would argue with that one. He says that focus and selection are what make wealthy investors. He is a billionaire [now the richest man in the world] and he invests in companies like Gillette [men will always need to shave unless we go back to the dark ages]. We agree with him here.

In the beginning of our investment career we were buying like it was going out of fashion. It was like there was a shortage and we did not want to miss out on the deals. We were addicted; there is no doubt about it, we jacked up on Property! We bought in Leeds, Bulgaria, Florida, Wellingborough and other areas near to Peterborough.

We were initially told that 'a deal is a deal' and it is 'good to buy all over to spread your portfolio far and wide.' Then we monitored and tested our portfolio. We compared the results, the costs and the pain-in-the-backside factor [official Progressive terminology]. They are all important and will all impact on your results and attitude towards your investments.

Our findings were this: anything that is more than 15 miles away from you is generally a pain and is not worth the hassle. The further we go out of our range, the more our investments cost us. The delays get longer. You lose control. When you go overseas you have legal and language barriers that hold things up all of the time.

And remember this: in Property, time is money. Something might look good on paper but the longer things take the more they cost. You can end up with big headaches and bigger bills the further afield you go.

There are Property deals everywhere, including somewhere near you. We shall talk more about your strategy later, and if you want to get someone else to help you. Let us assume that you are going to select your own area to invest.

This is how *not* to do it: guess. Pin the tail on the donkey [map]. Choose an area that was reported to be a 'hotspot' 2 years ago. Choose somewhere that you can't get to easily. Choose somewhere too expensive or too trendy. We could go on...

Before we talk about an area that you choose to invest in, let us talk about the UK in general. There is a lot of talk about the north/south divide and where is best to invest.

As we see it, if you live in Brighton, regardless of the huge growth that you might have heard about up north or in Scotland, you need to stick somewhere near your patch. We know many investors who are making awesome amounts of money in the south. Traditional thinking over the last few years has been that the yields are higher [cheaper houses] in the north. This may be true, and yes, there has been regeneration up north and towards Scotland, but everything needs to be taken into context. Gross yield and net yield are 2 very different things, and these things all happen in cycles.

The south seems to have been undergoing a 'revival' in growth over the last couple of years, when compared with the north. Some central areas in London grew at phenomenal rates [over 70% in a year] and the implication of the Olympics and other factors have had great short term impact.

What we are trying to tell you here is that you are always going to get crests in growth. There is always going to be a north/south argument. You are always going to get regeneration of certain areas. Be aware of this but don't get sucked in to chasing the elusive.

With all of this in mind, this is how you should be buying if you want maximum return with minimal effort; minimum pain, and minimum time and cost:

Rob Moore & Mark Homer

**Look at somewhere within about a 15 mile radius of you**: don't be pulled too far away from where you live. If you are happy to travel further then fine, and we know successful investors who do travel a little further. In areas around London it may be more difficult to find good yields and you may need to go out to areas like Milton Keynes or into Essex.

Use this as a guideline. [If you live in certain areas that may be too expensive or too run down you may have to travel further, in which case it just needs to be put in your strategy]. The main thing is to keep all of your investments close enough together so that they are manageable. The reasons are as stated and you will really be pleased you did when you start to buy more heavily. Remember focus.

**Look for investment, growth or regeneration**: when doing your diligence can you find areas that are being heavily redeveloped? There are many areas in the south that are going to have regeneration work due to the Olympics, and this can have an effect on growth. Surrounding areas can also experience the 'ripple effect' of regeneration.

Perhaps you know of masterplan redevelopments of specific areas? Peterborough is currently going through a **£1billion** redevelopment of a big part of the city. This will have a huge impact on the economics of the city, as well as the Property market [especially the little existing ones].

Look at industry and technology. Perhaps you know of large

companies relocating and creating jobs in a city. Many large companies have moved their offices out of London and further afield because of high prices there. This can create more money, jobs and need for housing within an area. Many areas within 100 miles of London have experienced this recently.

It is getting easier and easier to find out all of the information you need from your desk. With Google now there really is no excuse in not finding out everything you need to know. We just typed in 'Peterborough Council' into Google and found all the links we needed for the regeneration plan, 'Opportunity Peterborough', house price statistics and population statistics.

A good place to start is here: www.communities.gov.uk. Click housing or cities and regions, it is a great resource.

You really can go into a lot of detail here if you wish. You can look at the bars/restaurants/club scene. You can look for culture and history such as museums, galleries and theatres. Does the town/city attract a big sports fraternity? Are the many festivals and events that would attract people? Are there famous people or celebrities who are known to live in a certain area? Are there good transport links?

Remember that all of these are worth thinking about but analysis paralysis is a disease of momentum; don't get too hung up on the details, just be aware of them.

Rob Moore & Mark Homer

**Look at the prices**: what are properties selling for in your area? What are they on the market for? If you want to find out what prices properties are selling for visit www.rightmove.co.uk. This is a great resource. You can also use www.nethouseprices.co.uk, though we find Rightmove is more complete.

You should know what properties are selling for. This is the only true indicator of Property values. Forget 'desk-top' valuations and guess work. Even official valuations can be wrong by up to 10%. Be very wary of new build and Property club valuations.

Rightmove is also a great resource for prices that properties are put on the market at. This is essential information. If you find an area where properties are selling at considerably below the asking prices, then there might be something going on there that you want to be a part of. If they are all selling within a week for full asking you know to move on.

Keep an eye on what is happening on these websites. Are there properties that seem to have been on there for months? Are there reductions in asking prices? Is there anything that gives you a sniff that the market might give you some deals?

Make some spreadsheets and put in the data. The best way to work out an average is to do just that. We know that some of you will love spreadsheets and some of you will hate them. Get into the habit of using them; they become simple, fast and easy.

I [Rob] hated the thought of using a spreadsheet a few years ago. I used to see Mark's head buried in his computer with all these numbers and think that he was some kind of Melvyn. Well needless to say he got me into them and I have never looked back. I can tell you everything in numbers; how many hours I work a week, as an average per day, how many days per year worked, the amount of days worked as a percentage to not worked, the amount of hours that are income generating and so on and on and on.

I'm honestly not a geek. It really has helped me improve every area of my life. The whole area of our business and portfolio is monitored very carefully. If you want to improve your portfolio performance then you know what you need to do.

Back to house prices: jump in your car and drive around your area. Are there many for sale boards? Are there many in any one particular area? Are there many that seem to have been there for months? Keep checking regularly.

A great resource for values of towns and cities is www.upmystreet.com. There you can find the average price of the average house in a given city. This helps you work out average yields in an area by comparing prices in cities versus the rent you might achieve. Areas vary considerably and this is important. You should be looking for gross yields of 6% upwards.

Rob Moore & Mark Homer

**Is the market moving?** Much of what we have just explained will help you to get a feel for market movements. Speaking to estate agents and asking them straight will very often give you the best idea. Make sure they are local as markets move in micro-economies. Ask them if there are many properties selling? Ask them if many are selling cheap. If they are, what areas are they in? You can get all of this information out of them with some of your relationship expert skills you now have [and have always had].

**What are the general folk talking about?** Is there a demand for tenants? It is all very well having all of the above, but if your Property will not rent out in 3 months then forget it. Estate agents with their own lettings departments might give you information you need.

**You absolutely need to find yourself a good letting agent.** Your performance in any given area will depend upon it. Some things to look out for: are they proactive or lazy? Are they knowledgeable on specific areas within a town or city? Ask them straight about rents for certain places and see if they know the figures. You can always go back and check what they say on www.rightmove.co.uk.

Don't shortcut all of this. Don't take the word of a Property club. Find out for yourself. You are in control.

# Summary

Focus on one area for your portfolio no more than 15 miles from where you live. Be diligent and selective of your area, making sure that the area is good for deals. Don't get lured outside your patch, all the deals you need are right here on your doorstep.

Rob Moore & Mark Homer

# Choose Your Property carefully [buy existing]

We are now getting to the heart of what will really make you money in Property. As important as the area you choose is the Property type you select.

We will save the 'what not to invest in' for the next section, so keep all of your questions in your mind for then...

Based on our experience and our portfolio evidence you should only be buying existing Property [5 years old or older]. There are many reasons. Perhaps the most important reason is value.

**Price is what you pay, value is what you get**: price and value can vary significantly. You *will* become an expert at buying on value rather than price.

If you buy a Property that is 5 years old [or older] you are getting an habitable dwelling that is suitable for rent [provided you have done your diligence] that will cost considerably less than an equivalent new Property. Developers make their margins in new Property [much like the car forecourt scenario], and you are not buying at the best value at that point because you are giving a proportion of the cost to the developer.

Wait until that premium has disappeared and you are buying a Property where the value is at its optimum. The good thing about housing is that the value can last for 100's of years. If you were to buy a new computer today at £1500 it would probably be worth about £400 in 3 years time and worth next to nothing in 5-10 years. The optimum time to buy that computer would probably be after one year when the value had dropped because it was no longer new technology [and new technology had come out], but it was still useful and not out of date.

With Property you can buy 30, 60, even 100 year old properties and they still have relative value. They are still useful and useable; unlike 30 year old computers [Do they exist?]. My Spectrum ZX isn't even that old!

**Understand yield**: we have a whole section on this so we'll save the surprise. You should be looking for properties with 6% yield and above. That is gross yield. Knowing the difference between gross yield and net yield is fundamental [it seems many people who will sell you Property do not get this].

Properties in nice areas will be too expensive compared to the rent that you will be able to achieve, and so the gross yield will be low. Properties in slums might have an attractive gross yield but by the time you have replaced your windows 3 times, got rid of the graffiti and your Sat Nav [window smashed] has been pinched out of your car, you won't be left with much of that. More later.

**Be specific with your Property type**: there are many types of properties that you can buy, which only goes to make things potentially confusing. We have found, almost all of the time, that it is best to focus on a specific type that works best for you. If you have already found your 'niche' then great. If not, this next section will be very important and could save you time and money.

In any one Property expo or show, for example, you could buy land for planning, land for development, developments, overseas holiday homes, off plan, self build, auctions, rent to buy, rent to own, Buy to Let, buy to sell, new build flats, shared ownership, repossessions, HMO's, commercial, existing single let Property. We could go on. You get the picture.

The choice can be quite nauseating. What we are discussing in this book is single let existing properties. Many of the above are unproven or need specific expertise far beyond buying regular houses for a much worse return. We focus on single let existing property because it is proven, it works, and more importantly to us, it's easy, it's replicable and it's scalable.

5 bed houses and 2 bed flats are very different investment propositions. What works best in terms of exact Property type will vary from area to area. In Peterborough studio, 1 & 2 bed flats and 2 & 3 bed semi's in certain areas work very nicely. We know that in other areas 2 bed flats or period conversions work the best for yield, rental coverage and grow relatively quickly. We've still not found any areas where MTV crib houses provide a good yield. You will discover what works best in your area. Once you know it, stick to what works best and don't mess about with anything too expensive or too far out of what you

now know to work.

Generally speaking, the properties at the cheaper end of the market will give you the best yields and are more likely to cover the mortgage payment with your rental income. The higher you go the less likely this is to happen.

With the lower end of the market you are buying properties that a bigger share of the market wants [or needs]. How many people out there do you think want to rent 6 bedroom houses? Of course there aren't many people who can afford 6 bed houses, and those that can are more likely to buy than rent.

The lower end offers far more demand. It also offers more long staying tenants. Newer and bigger properties attract transient families and single career minded people. Many of our tenants have never moved from our smaller existing properties as they will be in similar circumstances for most of their life. They are much less likely to buy as they may not be able to afford the deposits or have good enough credit to get reasonable mortgage products. They have a 'rental mindset' as that is the way they have been brought up. These are the kinds of tenants you want in your properties.

It is quite important to explain this 'rental mentality.' You or I may always have aspirations to buy one or many houses, as we understand the benefits, have the knowledge to get a mortgage and a belief that we can either afford it now, or sometime in the not too distant future.

However, when dealing with people near the lower end of the market, things are very different. Knowledge, experience and education are lower in general, and the belief that one day they may be able to actually to buy a house is very often never there, because their perception is that it will always be too expensive. It is also quite common for these people to see buying other 'things' [beer, Plasma TV's, the latest trainers] as more important.

These people still want a home and still want their home to feel like their home, whether they physically own it or not. We've never really experienced the common myths about properties getting trashed because we find that the tenants that we deal with have the belief that the house they rent is the house that they own; that it is *their* home. This is a great thing to understand when renting a Property, especially when compared to the professional rental mentality which is transient because they will look to buy as soon as possible or move frequently with their job.

Very often tenants are on DSS [DHSS] whose rents [or a greater portion of their rent] are being paid by the council. This is regular guaranteed rent and can be a great option. Again, this will be up to you to find out for your particular area.

Rob Moore & Mark Homer

## Summary

Be very selective of your Property type and stick to that one type for all of your investments. Don't buy anything new, overseas or off plan. Stick to the lower end of the market and what works well in your area for net yield, rental coverage and growth.

# Don't buy anything else

Remember our discussions about focus, strategy and delaying gratification? Well we hope you can [it was only 15 minutes ago].

Having bought many properties of many different types, we want you to know the truth, from our experience, about Property investment and what will work best for you.

This is our experience and our opinion. In different areas and with particular expertise, most things can potentially be made to work. You are of course reading this book and we want to see you in the right direction.

This is what we have discovered, and in particular what you should avoid. You should be aware and particularly wary of [what most Property clubs and new build companies **do not** tell you about most Property investments]:

**Discounts**: most Property 'clubs' or companies who offer new build, off plan and overseas Property are sourcing Property for you that have false or 'paper' discounts.

A real discount is one that is below the market value of a Property that can be proved with comparables [evidenced]; that is the same type of Property in the same area sold for the same price in the same resale market. **Not** a price that a financially unsophisticated first time buyer has paid, which included the developer paying their 5% deposit: with carpet, curtains, free light fittings and a Plasma TV thrown in!

If the company can show you a similar house on a similar road that has sold previously at that price, then it is worth that price. However most will only give you speculative 'desk-top' [off-plan] valuations [guesses or valuations that they want] and forward priced properties. Even if these valuations have been 'proven' by a 'RICS' surveyor, be wary. If there are no comparables for properties of the same type in the same resale market then it is guess work, not just for you but for a surveyor too [we learned that the expensive way].

**Off-Plan and New Build**: buying off-plan and new build Property is just like buying a new Mercedes straight from the forecourt. As soon as you drive it away you have lost 10-20% of its value.

There are optimum points in the purchase of any object where the residual values are at their optimum; the point at which the relative value is at the greatest level. You can buy a brand New Range Rover for almost £70,000, and you can buy a 4 or 5 year old one for £15,000. The model is exactly the same, no facelift, no improved models; still the same model in the same cycle.

If you had bought that brand new and fancy Range Rover you would have lost almost £55,000 in 4 to 5 years. For the next 4 to 5 years that car will lose much less value because the residuals are much better at this point.

Property is exactly the same. When you buy a new Property you are paying a premium: you are paying over the odds so that the developer can take their profit. This is fair enough, the developer is in business and needs to make a bob or two, but the Property clubs will tell you they have gone out and 'sourced' a 'genuine 15% discount.'

There is one big difference between buying a car and a Property, and that is that there are very few cars that go up in value over time, whereas there are very few properties that go down in value over time. However the residual concept is no different.

Let's look at this relatively and go back a few years. Yes, right now, we don't think that new build Property works on cash flow. It can often take much longer to grow and can cost you money on a monthly basis. We have regularly heard of shortfalls of £200 - £500 per month.

When BTL first started to become 'popular,' around the mid to late 90's, there were bargains to be had in the new build arena. You could perhaps buy a Property right at the start of a development, and get it for the cheapest price, and by the time the whole development was finished, perhaps in 2nd or 3rd phase, the new prices would drag the value of your flat upwards.

This did happen.

And perhaps if you were to time your purchase just right, at the very end of the development, you could get a flat or two when developers needed desperately to report to shareholders with sales figures, where they might let the last couple go cheaper than 'market value.'

This is certainly what you will be told you can achieve through buying new Property, and perhaps it has been done. However we are more than 10 years on from this, and everything that is now new that we have ever seen is always at a premium.

The fundamental flaw with this strategy is that it is totally dependent on a rising market. The truth seems to be that rising markets can actually 'smooth over' poorly purchased investment properties; this has definitely been our personal experience. However they will only do this whilst the market is rising a good 15-20% per year, and in reality this is not sustainable over the long term.

There will be other periods of time where the market rises heavily, and we should all look forward to that when we have built a good portfolio, but we must never rely on it to make money.

**Fundamental tip No.7:
We must rely on our ability to buy well whatever the market is

doing. You make your money when you buy.

The developers and 'clubs' now throw all sorts of 'incentives' your way to try to lure you in, and hide the reality that has become easier to spot in a market that may not be as 'bull.' This is especially the case as things have changed over the last 10 years or so.

Free carpets, curtains, upgraded appliances, car parking spaces, cash-backs, guaranteed rentals, gifted deposits, stamp duty paid are all hooks to reel you in. None of these have an impact on the value of the Property. None of these all of a sudden [as if by magic] make an over-priced [for investment] new-build Property a bargain.

Very often a '15% discount' in new build Property actually equates to buying the Property at near its real value [so you have in fact gained no discount whatsoever].

Perhaps this is all about understanding the difference between what you would buy because you really want it, and what you would buy to make money.

It does however mean that you can often buy with little or no deposit – the only advantage. This means that the bank is taking an increased risk. It generally also means that your rent will nowhere near cover your mortgage and full costs. You will be paying up to £500 per month to keep these properties! No thanks.

**Why Developers have the Last Laugh**: developers are not stupid. They are in the business of making money and are not just going to give their products and profit margins away. They know that there are hundreds of 'Property clubs' and new build companies out there who are desperate for properties with 'genuine discounts' to sell to their large database of unsuspecting investors. That is good news for them.

Developers charge premium rates for their new developments. We have personally seen a specific example in Peterborough where developers are offering 2 bed flats at the same price as older 4 bed houses opposite that are *twice* the square footage. It is insane.

Older properties that have 'settled' offer better value because that developers' premium has gone. Some S-class Mercedes' were £100,000 when new and are now worth £30,000 3 years later. The same happens to new Property, so why not buy it at £30,000 instead of £100,000 where the residual value is much better?!

**Rate of growth**: in addition to this [and in our very own personal experience] not only will you buy a Property that you think is discounted that in reality is not, but your new build Property will then likely not go up for another 3 years or so.

Taking the example in Peterborough that we have just given

you, in 10 years the larger existing house could quite easily be worth double, perhaps somewhere around the £350-£400K mark. A new flat that is now not new [because there are many other trendy new developments popping up everywhere] will have not gone up anywhere near as much. The market will have to even out and become relative.

If you compare older properties in the same area, then like for like will cost you around the same money, give or take a few pence. However if you compare a Property that is a 4 bed house next to a Property that is a 2 bed flat in the same area, then the house could be up to 100% more money.

The average value of a 2 bed flat in Peterborough today, according to www.home.co.uk, is between £131,907 and £140,332 but the average value of a 4 bed house is £245,820!

Buy a new build flat and it is likely that in 10 years it could be worth a little over half that of the 4 bed house, yet you are paying the same money for it now. *Just don't do it*. It does not make long term sense.

**Why Memberships are unfair and unnecessary**: what are you paying for? What 'service' is being provided by a 'membership' to an 'exclusive Property club?' You are paying for the privilege of lining someone else's pockets as you are not receiving a service for your money.

**Overseas properties and holiday homes**: this can be a real minefield. There are so many companies offering these dreams and it can all get very tempting. The marketing, the sun, the seascapes, the white flowing clothes on the beach, the super slow-mo, the big shaggy dogs and the dreamy lifestyle pictures all make us think about being somewhere hot and idyllic...

But wait: before you get carried away there. Back in the room...

The mistake that many first-time investors make is that they confuse a holiday home or overseas dream with profitable Property investment. If you want a second home abroad to live in at certain time of the year, then this is fine, but don't expect it to make any money at all for a long time. Expect it to cost you year on year and expect to get a few headaches; maybe even the odd heart attack! Many people get their emotions entangled with the concepts of investment and ultimately end up spending vast amounts of money for very little return.

**Fundamental tip No.8:
Buy on logic, not emotion.

The deal is all about the numbers. Love the numbers if they work. Don't love the carpet and the wallpaper, the curtains or the gated video entrance; love the numbers.

You can make overseas Property investment work if you're an expert, if you live in the country you want to invest in and you know the area like your own town or city. You'll need to be able to speak the language, have a large contact base and know the intricacies of the legal system [and the differences from the UK market].

We've been talking a lot in this book about rules. The rules of Property investment are so different from country to country. It can take years to learn the rules for our own country, let alone other foreign speaking countries hundreds and thousands of miles away.

The reason that we tell people to steer well clear of any overseas Property is because of all of the above. It's just so much time and hassle; too many variables can go wrong for us and turn profit into dust. None of us are ever likely to be any of the above. It's actually far easier to be an expert [or just good] in our own areas.

We speak from experience here. We know people who are paying **£100,000** cash for overseas Property in places like Cyprus. Just imagine that. How many properties could you buy in the UK with that money? Places like that will only rent out for a few weeks of the year and you have no control over your money. *Just don't do it*.

In our early years we invested overseas. We were allured by big promises of capital gains. However, rentals frequently didn't match up to promises and mortgages were extremely difficult to obtain. Values did not rise as expected and most properties were inflated because they were new. Then, to top this, the language and legal barriers were [and still are] a complete nightmare.

There will always be news of the latest hotspot and the next big thing abroad. By the time we hear about it on the street it is probably too late. Companies will flog them as long as they can to get the maximum profit out of the 'hype.' We tend to ignore all of this. Yes there will be some far away market that grows 50% in one year, but finding it would be more luck than judgement. The market is likely to be quite volatile, and in the long run the average will even out. And remember we are looking at long term financial independence here.

In case you are still thinking of buying a Property from a 'club' be aware [wary] of the following: a Property company should perform, provide and do the following if you want to feel happy and secure about your investments:

**Proper diligence of a deal that they supply**: most of them don't and when pushed do not know enough about the development. If you hear 'well if the deal works, the deal works,' when you discuss numbers, be very suspicious.

**Proper financial analysis**: we believe it is a duty of care for a Property company to tell you the full costs of your investment, not just rent vs. mortgage, or what they see relevant to their responsibilities [i.e. not much].

**Evidence**: many figures such as values and rental predictions are exactly that: predictions [guesses]. Demand evidence to avoid disappointment.

**Support**: most Property clubs do not want to know as soon as you have paid them your 'finders' fee. Unless you have bought many properties before, you will be lumbered with one big headache because [in the beginning especially], you will need help and guidance; financially, logistically and emotionally.

**Invest in their product themselves**: but be careful here. We have personally met directors who will buy their products but use your money to fund the huge shortfalls and costs.

**Leverage**: a Property company should save you time [years if they are good] in sourcing you a good Property with a genuine evidenced discount [and equity] from day one. They should use their experience and knowledge and manage a process for you, from finding the Property all through to acquiring and managing a tenant. So why do most of them just want to sell you a Property [regardless of cost] and leave you to fend for yourself? If you have not purchased many properties before then be aware of this.

Sorry if all of this seems a little negative but we want you to know the truth as we see it. We don't want you to make a big mistake early on in your investment career and be burned for life. We hope that this helps and makes you aware of the

Rob Moore & Mark Homer

potential pitfalls in Property investing.

At the same time this should not put you off. Knowing the truth will massively increase your chances of building a steady and secure long term Property portfolio that will look after you for the rest of your life, and for generations to come.

We've been there, and now you don't have to.

## Summary

Don't be sucked in by the big promises of most Property clubs. New build, off plan and overseas Property will, more often than not, cost you more money and give you much more pain than existing Property in your area. Stick to your strategy and reap the rewards for the mid – long term.

# Buy at discount [make money when You buy]

**Fundamental tip No.9:
You make your money when you buy.

This is an age old Property cliché that is so important. When you master the Art of getting true BMV [Below Market Value] Property then your Property investment success will multiply.

There are obvious reasons for getting good discounts: you save money and you get something worth more than you paid for it. Of course. But they are not the only benefits.

A very important point is that if you can get yourself a nice evidenced 15-30% discount [and sometimes better] then you know that the market can go down 15 or 20% and you are safe. You will not be in negative equity and you have a comfortable buffer. We happen to think this is important.

It is this Art that separates would-be or novice investors [some with plenty of money] from specialist and expert investors. There are many investors we know who are buying properties for cash and buying them at full market value. Yes they will make money in the long run because most of us will in Property, but they could be making up to 10 times what they are making just using some skill, knowledge and experience.

Having discussed new build discounts and everything that you should not be doing to achieve your discount, why don't we talk

Rob Moore & Mark Homer

about how you can actually find these great deals. Is that ok with you?

Glad to hear it.

**It's a numbers game**: we discussed this earlier. Specific to achieving discounts, you need to be putting the offers in to get the deals you want. Putting in one or two offers that are rejected and then giving up is not going to make you rich. We get one deal in approximately 8 offers through estate agents that we feel has a big enough discount. We get about one deal per 5000 leaflets that are posted out [from around 9 phone calls] and we are improving all of the time.

Put in the offers, play the numbers game and you will get the deals. If you don't shoot, you don't score.

**Be patient**: don't go negotiation crazy. Know your price that you want to pay and don't budge. If your offer gets rejected then wait, be patient, and in 3 months when expectations have levelled, you may well get some offers back your way.

This actually happens quite frequently for us. In fact just recently I [Mark] helped an investor buy a flat. We actually went to look at it nearly 4 months ago and the vendor was adamant that he wanted [and was going to get] full asking price. We just waited and the market picked away at him and now we have helped her get the flat for around £30,000 less than the original asking price. The vendor is also happy because he needs to move fast and has had people pull out on previous offers.

We also know some bullish hot-headed 'dealmakers' who try to bully people on price and pressure on time. The people we speak to on the other end of those negotiations don't like it at all and it doesn't work.

**Always be improving**: keep improving on your figures. Keep learning, reading, growing, becoming a relationship expert and testing your results so that you know what you can improve on: this is most important.

**Use different marketing methods**: use estate agents, use leaflets, use websites and Google Adwords, use word of mouth, use print media. More than one strategy will bring many more deals than just a single one.

**Stick to what you know**: now that you have decided on area and type of Property, stick to it. You will become known for what you want by agents and they will come to you with what you want. If you chase everything and buy outside your strategy then you won't get the results you want.

We bought a bungalow last year [outside our strategy] because we got something like an 18% discount. Nice at first but then it took nearly 5 months to refurb, and when it came to renting it out, the figures were nowhere near what our others were producing. We knew we shouldn't have bought it, so we sold it. It is the only Property in our portfolio that we have sold.

Rob Moore & Mark Homer

However that is better than not buying at all. Those who chase everything get a reputation for being good at nothing and deals will run away from them.

**Know your numbers**: this is one of the most important factors in buying a Property. Before you even put an offer in you should know exactly what that Property will cost you to buy, including *all* fees. You should know what the rental figures are and what it will cost you per month with a contingency put in. If you have built a good relationship with a good letting agent then they will help you with rental figures. There is no excuse here.

**Yield**: there are many other factors that you will need to understand, such as the areas within your area that offer the best yield. There are always little pockets within towns and cities that offer the best net yield. Some areas will be too expensive and some will be too cheap [with high maintenance]. Unfortunately we cannot help you with any area outside of Peterborough. We have focused and become experts in this one area. You will have to learn this yourself if you want to become a successful and profitable Property investor [we can't do everything for you!].

**Watch interest rates**: as interest rates creep up more people [especially in the lower end of the market] get into more financial difficulties because the repayments on their loans go up. More repossessions happen at this point and you can use all of your newly acquired skills as a relationship expert to lead them out of debt and pick up a bargain. More detail later on.

**Timing is everything**: in Property buying timing is everything. If you can understand when the best time to buy is by keeping your eye on the market, then you are one step ahead of 95% of Property investors.

Our second book is all about making money when the market isn't moving upwards. It is far better to buy at these times that in a bull and rising market. You can make massive profits now:

www.progressiveproperty.co.uk/book2-buy-now.asp

Certain times of year dictate buying prices. For example, most people are not prepared to buy over Christmas as it is a huge upheaval. However you do, in some cases, get people who really need to sell quickly, and because there is not much going on, you can benefit. Summertime can be interesting too. If a lot of people are on holiday then this can obviously have a real impact on what is happening in the market.

**Know what makes vendors tick**: understanding the psychology of your vendor [seller] will make a huge impact on the prices you get. You should always be thinking about getting as much information from the vendor [sometimes through an agent] as possible. Do they have to move quickly? Are they in debt? Is it a probate sale? Do they have bad neighbours [perhaps you should stay away]? Has their Property been on the market for 3 months or more? Is there a chain in the sale? Could you help find them a new house? The more you know the more *leverage* you have to negotiate.

Rob Moore & Mark Homer

**Follow all the previous rules**: don't buy new, focus on area and Property type, understand finance and be ready to buy fast with your broker ready and your DIP [decision in principle] in place. Never ever pull out of a deal, have the other person's interest in mind, offer value and give them something.

Now go out and find some great deals!

**Keep going**; make mistakes. So what. We all make them. If you don't shoot, you don't score [and that doesn't just go for football and members of the opposite sex!] It's all part of your growth to becoming a seriously profitable and successful Property investor. I [Rob; of course it wouldn't be Mark] once spent £600 [I didn't have] on a pair of cowboy boots. I now know you can get a nice vintage pair from Camden for £60. Idiot.

Mistakes are essential in learning to be good at anything. It is said that those who make the most mistakes become the best. Remember Thomas Edison? It is the learning and the meaning we put on the mistakes that we make that make us who we are, both as investors and people.

"Anyone who has never made a mistake has never tried anything new." Albert Einstein.

**Enjoy the process**: hunting for deals should be fun. It is a game and we love it. You can get out there, help other people sell their house faster than anyone else and make some money yourself. You are not gazumping people or flying in like vultures, you are setting up win-win scenarios and loving it. At least we do and you should too.

Remember the story Mark told at the beginning?!

## Summary

Buy at evidenced discount and you will make money from day one. The better the discount you get, the more of a safety net you will have. Remember that you are creating 'win-wins' by helping vendors to desired outcomes.

# The Art of finance & borrowing money

Your ability to obtain credit is paramount to the exponential growth of your portfolio.

Before we even start on this chapter always remember this: *guard your credit score with your life*. Nurture and protect it like a child. Cushion it. Wrap your arms around it and never let it go.

Never ever miss a mortgage payment and always keep well up to date with what you owe. One missed payment can black mark your credit and hinder future lending, and the growth of your portfolio.

This is your map. Without the map you will never find the treasure. Pull out all the clichés: this is the genie in your lamp. If you remember nothing else in this book; remember this. This is your golden ticket to the chocolate factory.

So you get that bit. When borrowing money consider your strategy very carefully indeed. When thinking about borrowing money there are 'Laws' that wealthy people follow. They follow these for good reason and they can easily be adopted into your strategy.

Because we all start from different places; and where you are is just where you ought to be, some of the following may not be relevant to your current position. But you never know when you may need to draw on these 'Laws':

**Only ever borrow from friends or family if you really must.** Borrowing from friends and family can put a strain on the relationships that are close to you. You will always be trying to avoid those who you owe money to, they will always be trying to catch up with you and friendships can be strained or lost because of that.

If you have a family member who owns a Property, this is very different. If they have equity, lend them this book. No, even better, buy them their own copy of this book. Be the tooth fairy and put it under their pillow. Let them read for themselves what they can do.

Jo Rhodes Lewis bought 4 for her friends for no reason at all; thank you Jo, it meant a lot to us:

www.progressiveproperty.co.uk/book-buy-now.asp

Even better still, we'll give you a free copy of "Make Cash in a Property Market Crash" if you tell 10 friends about this book. We are now in the recommendation age. If you believe that you could take *just one* thing from this book and make *just one* change that was worth £20 then we would love to help your friends and loved ones do the same now.

We've made it very easy for you too. All you have to do is log on to the web address below, copy the text that is on the page into an email and send it to 10 of your friends that you believe may benefit from the value that we believe can make you £100,000's.

You will also need to copy us in to the email so that we can see that you are not just trying to get a cheeky free book for doing nothing!

www.progressiveproperty.co.uk/email.asp

Don't forget to copy us in and use the text on the page:

robmoore@progressiveproperty.co.uk

**Only break the Law of borrowing from friends and family if you absolutely positively must**. And then make sure you do. In this scenario, when you have invested everything you have into something you truly believe in, you absolutely do what you *have* to do to make it work.

We did and never looked back, and this is the *only* exception to borrowing from friends and family [many of them, having been paid back, will feel good about being able to have helped in your successful venture].

If it is sink or swim then blow up your orange wings and start doggy paddling!

Rob Moore & Mark Homer

**Only borrow to invest in income producing assets.**
There are many schools of thought [particularly that of the Industrial age], that you should never spend anything until you have it, and never borrow money. This is a sound base on which to build a solid financial platform, and certainly far better than borrowing to buy petrol guzzling cars, go on fancy cruises and build conservatories.

Never ever borrow money to invest in liabilities until you can afford to do so. If you can afford them, then why are you borrowing money for them in the first place? If there is a cost of capital then fair enough. If not, then buy it with spare cash that you can afford to lose.

The same goes for Property. We have seen many people gearing up [borrowing] to 90% on Buy to Let mortgages to get some cash back or reduce the amount of money they put in a Property deal. Most of this is on the recommendation of Property clubs and it scares us silly to be honest.

Extra borrowing over and above what you need is extra **debt**. It is debt that you have to pay off. If you have leveraged up too much and you now have a shortfall [extra payments on top of your rental income] of a few hundred pounds per month, then this will hurt as the cash-back will soon run out.

It might be presented that a cash-back can pay the shortfall but it won't last very long and the debt will still be there. Imagine a Property upside down by £500 per month [yes we know companies offering this] when taking into account realistic costs. Then multiply that by 10, 20 or 50, it can really start to hurt. Is that what you want for your portfolio?

We don't. And we know you don't have to, if you buy well and follow the strategies in this book.

No one ever set up a big business, however, without borrowing money. Most people could never buy a house unless they borrowed money. There can be great leverage in borrowing money to create something that could potentially generate a lifetime of income far beyond the repayments.

So again, you have all the warnings, which is very important.

80% of this game is **money**. It is about extracting the maximum lending from a bank so that you can get the most Property with the least amount of your money, remembering the factors just discussed.

This comes down to having a good broker who understands how these deals work. Forget high street banks, forget standard high street brokers; get a specialist who is fast, efficient and knows how to make things fit to get you a mortgage.

A fallacy that I [Mark] hear quite a lot is

"I can't get a mortgage."

Absolute rubbish. People can get mortgages from the day that they step out of bankruptcy [it will just be at a higher rate]. Buy to Let mortgages are the easiest thing in the world to obtain. Most lenders will let you self certify your income [and many don't even require you to have much income anyway] if you have problems getting evidence because you are self employed.

Age is not an issue either, I got a Buy to Let mortgage for someone who was 84 last year; the broker just had to find the right lender.

Slightly off the subject but something that bugs me a bit are the stories you read in the newspapers about first time buyers not being able to get on the housing ladder because they can't get a mortgage. This is clearly complete nonsense, as there are a whole stack of lenders out there that will provide almost anyone with a mortgage. A mortgage is finance secured on just about the most stable, sure and secure asset in the world – Property!

Instead of moaning about how our young can't afford to buy why don't we give them some financial education? Why not teach them how to buy a house at an early age?

Teach them how to live in a room and rent the others out to pay the mortgage. This model still works in most parts of the country even with a really small deposit. If they can't afford a deposit we will show them a couple of ways to buy a Property with no deposit – just contact Mark at markhomer@progressiveproperty.co.uk

Teach them to delay gratification. Stop giving them squillions on credit cards at 25% and teach them how to raise finance properly. End of rant!

Surveyors form a key part in the financial process. Again, you should try and make these guys your friends. Build rapport. Use your relationship skills. Read the section on estate agents and apply the same principles. Be honest with them.

Try to make their job easier by providing them with information on the Property like the location of garages, construction type, perhaps some comparables and so on.

I have attended many surveys over the years and have had good and bad experiences. A surveyor's job is to provide a report on the suitability of the Property for lending purposes, and will usually be there on behalf of the lender, not you or me! Their main aim is to gain instructions [fees] for surveys whilst protecting themselves and their insurance company against having to pay out as the result of professional negligence.

I have found different surveyors to value a Property wildly differently [as much as 25% in some cases], especially on new build sites, as asset valuation is subjective and relies on an element of opinion. This is why they generally have a 5% - 10% accepted margin in these valuations. With this in mind you can potentially control the situation to your benefit.

Rob Moore & Mark Homer

Generally on existing properties which have been around for a while in a stable market, values are more accurate than on new build sites where developer/Property club will often give buyer incentives that try to mask *real value*.

Surveyors should usually value a Property based on comparable sold properties in the area. This does not necessarily mean properties that have completed – so it can be properties that estate agents have got going through at that time. In my experience it is best to try and use a different surveyor for the valuation of the Property for the first purchase mortgage from the mortgage [remortgage] that you obtain 3 or 4 months later for the revaluation of a Property.

This would happen if you are following our strategy to buy cheap, add value through refurbishment, and then get your money back.

There is a very specific reason for this. Surveyors will often just look at what they valued a Property a few months before. They may add a small amount on to protect themselves, rather than giving it the full value based on the comparables. It is as though they are refusing to accept that you have bought the Property cheaply at less than it was worth!

Another tip is to use a 'mean' valuer [you will work out who they are!] for the initial purchase and a 'generous' one for the remortgage. It's all about people remember.

As they build up confidence in you they are likely to accept more of what you say, and value properties more generously. They will realise that it won't come back on them because you are in the 'game' of Property and are unlikely to be repossessed.

A little method I learned from a friend which works really well: when you own a significant portion of a building or street [and you will], as we do with our portfolio, you can effectively control the perceived value of these properties yourself.

Say you had a Property which needed to be valued at a certain price along a street on which you owned several properties. You could put the ones you own up for sale with agents you know for £10k-£20k more than they are 'worth,' just like I did in my early days of investing on a particular street in Peterborough.

When the Property gets valued you now have a load of properties in the same street/area to compare at the higher value. You have also just raised the value of the properties on the street by this amount. The neighbours and agents will see your prices and not accept less for their properties!

A similar concept can be applied to lettings – if you want to raise your rents get a few letting agents to advertise your existing properties at £100 a month more than they are 'worth' [you may need to assure your existing tenants that you're just doing market research or something]. You will find that you will have set a new rental level in the building or street. Clever eh? Fun? Oh yes.

So how can you apply all of this knowledge now?

The equity in your own home, for example, could potentially be used to purchase a further 5 or 10 properties with a little help from the bank. Borrowing money here with one simple transaction that shouldn't have very much impact on your current finances, [if done correctly] can set you up for life.

It is this simple: if you believe that you have an investment opportunity that will return greater income than the cost of the loan repayments, then you should be borrowing money to invest.

Some numbers again for you [a typical example]:
Your house worth £250,000
Your current mortgage £100,000
Your capital repayments £700 pcm [approx]
Your equity: £150,000

Let's look at what some simple refinancing can do for you:

Your remortgage: [85% of £250,000] £212,500
Your old mortgage paid off leaving cash: £112,500
Your new interest only repayments: £1325 pcm [approx]

Money to re-invest: *£112,500*

Your typical strategy:

Bank £30,000 for your increase in mortgage for over 3 years

Bank £23,000 as a contingency

Invest £59,500: 5 properties

Now let's compare the results:

Your house on your old mortgage: £250,000 going up at 10% per year: £25,000 [compounding - going up year on year].

Your new portfolio:

6 properties [your house plus 5 investments]: £1,000,000 [conservative estimate of your Property plus 5 properties in 6 years] going up at 10% per year: *£100,000* [compounding - going up year on year].

For 10 years of compounded growth figures, go to page 383 at the back of the book.

And for the first 3 and a half years that has cost you absolutely nothing, and you still have a £25,000 contingency. After year 3 when the shortfall payments have run out you can remortgage should you wish. The cost of living would have gone up; your rents should have gone up, so that shortfall will be [relatively] much less in real terms.

Understanding finance is everything. This is a nice basic representation of what you can quite easily do on what you

Rob Moore & Mark Homer

have got already, without having to go out and get a second job or rob a bank!

We've used many creative finance strategies in our time to maximise leverage and buy Property with as little or no money at all.

Just remember that understanding finance will mean, quite simply: you can **buy more with less**. You could even **buy much more with nothing at all**.

## Summary

Understand the Art of finance and how you can use borrowed money to earn infinite returns on your money. If you have equity sitting idle in your house now then look at how you can leverage that for 10 times the return straight away.

# Never sell

Amongst the most savvy and serious residential Property investors, never selling a Property is generally regarded as the best strategy. Perhaps we could have put this in section 2, but now is a good time to discuss this.

This actually shocks, surprises, mystifies and confuses many people. However when they get this concept, everything changes for them and everything becomes clear and easy. At Progressive Property we have a view that we should all do what works for us, following certain 'Laws' or guidelines, which we are discussing with you here.

If you buy well, and make your money when you buy [as previously mentioned], then this 'Law' applies 100% for asset building purposes: for building your 5, 10 or 20+ Property portfolio. It should be obvious that if you buy and sell, you never actually grow a portfolio, you just tread water. You are slaying the Golden Goose; you are chopping down the Golden apple tree. However it is not always that obvious to some.

You will never become massively wealthy turning properties around on this scale. It is generally too time intensive, there are too many variables that can go against you, low ROI's, one off payments as opposed to being paid forever, and very high disposal costs.

The key to your investment strategy is to know what you want to achieve and then work your investments around that. Your strategy will be becoming ever more clear now.

Do bear this in mind. If you are looking for cash flow, and you are cash-flow poor, then buying properties [on a single let with an 85% mortgage] and holding them will not generate cash flow in the short term. Remember that we are talking about a **mid-long term** strategy here. One that works. One that will last your whole life. One that will cost you the minimum amount of money for the maximum return.

We personally know people who make some cash flow from turning properties around; that is to buy and sell them at a 'profit.' Of course this is what they tell us, but most people only tell us what they want us to know, don't they? Before we go into building an asset base, let us look at why someone might sell [and their 'strategy'] and you can make your own assumptions based on this.

In order to successfully 'flip' properties, or buy and sell at a profit that is worthwhile, you really do need to know what you are doing. There are so many factors that could go wrong. Just watch the whole host of Property programmes on TV and see how the average non-investor fares. Do not follow the TV strategy; it's dumbed down and it is not indicative of reality. It's just daytime candy-fodder.

Without going into great detail, matters such as planning, legislation and legal work, building work, timing, gearing, market research, sourcing, people and negotiation skills and contact base are all of vital importance in effectively selling a Property at profit.

There are very few people who can make that work and it is a very time intensive strategy. Most of these people using this strategy think they are making far more money than they actually are because of the true cost of turning a Property around. A £200,000 Property will actually cost you around £17,000 in fees. There is most [if not all] of your profit gone. We have had to point this out many times to 'Property traders' as they didn't even realise themselves how much the costs spiral and eat profits.

Here are the actual costs of buying and selling a Property, from personal experience [average figures]:

£100,000 Property example:

Buying costs: £2,500
[broker fees, solicitor fees, valuation fees, lending costs, admin and disbursements]

Selling costs: £8,000
[void periods, valuation, agency fees, solicitors and legal fees, insurances, admin and disbursements]

Total Cost: £10,500

Rob Moore & Mark Homer

This is most, if not all of your potential profit, and does not even include any refurb costs. This can easily turn into £15,000 plus.

It's even worse on a £200,000 Example:

Buying costs: £4,500
[broker fees, solicitor fees, valuation fees, lending costs, admin and disbursements]

Selling costs: £13,000
[void periods, valuation, agency fees, solicitors and legal fees, insurances, admin and disbursements]

Stamp Duty: £2,000

Total Cost: £19,500

And to cap it all off, they no longer own the asset which is now making money for someone else! So if you would like to follow that strategy, then good luck in your new full time job working 65 hours per week for little reward and no long term value.

Another point of note here is HMO, or letting properties out by the room. We own a few, and they do cash flow on paper. What most people will not tell you is the cost implication. This very much varies depending on your area. In Peterborough you will need around £22,000 to buy an HMO and get it ready to let, including deposit and changes for regulation, such as fire doors and emergency lighting. That is £22,000 that is tied up and 'stays in' the Property. It's also a real pain in the neck. And the backside. And a big cost of capital.

If you think that we can buy existing single let properties, do our magic, get all of our money back out through refurb and remortgage; that is an infinite return on investment. If an HMO cash-flows at about £400 per month then you will pay tax on that income and it will take over 5 years to get your money back that you've left in.

It is very difficult to get any kind of discount on big HMO's in our area on a specific model that works well for investment purposes. There are investors who don't understand leverage who are gobbling them up at full asking price. And we're not talking about new build HMO's at £180,000 here [you know to stay well clear of those, don't you?]. We are talking about Property that we can buy at around £125,000 that really does make you £400 per month, after *all* costs.

You don't get that equity from day one like you can with the single lets [it's all in the way you buy – the evidenced discounts]. Can you see how and why strategy becomes so important now?

Building assets that you can get at discount to leverage your money will generate you mid-long term wealth. It is this mindset, rather than instant gratification, that will guide you to financial success in your portfolio.

This is why we believe you must **Never** sell your properties:

Rob Moore & Mark Homer

1. Your valuable asset now belongs to someone else
2. That someone else earns on your valuable asset for the rest of their life
3. It costs around £19,500 to buy and sell a house worth £200,000
4. You no longer earn on that valuable asset (Get the picture?)
5. You don't pay 40% capital gains tax on your Property if you never sell it
6. You can gain higher valuation of your Property through remortgage (selling incurs many costs and you rarely get 100% of the value of your Property when you sell)
7. You compound your earnings as you build a portfolio. You cannot do this if you keep selling your properties

Of course there are exceptions, as there are to every 'rule.' If you've bought a 'kipper' [structurally defective, damp issues, lease problems, huge shortfalls, above a kebab shop, in a war zone] then by all means get rid of it if you think it will serve you better. Learn your lesson [like we did] and move on; fast.

You wouldn't believe how many people we talk with wish they had not sold their house 5 years ago: people who tell us that their old house is now worth *double* what it was 5 years ago.

Would you like some figures? It is this simple:

You own one house that is worth £200,000 [example: insert your own figures here]. That will go up £20,000 per year tax free [compounding - going up year on year] at 10% growth.

You build an asset base following the rules: 10 houses worth £200,000 each = £2million. Your portfolio will go up **£200,000** per year tax free [compounding - going up year on year] at 10% growth.

If your strategy involves using other people's time [leverage] and other people's money [leverage] for long term financial gain and independence, then the strategy of never selling is a **must** for you.

If you have an asset [your house] with equity in it, then make sure you keep it. If you need cash to re-invest and buy more 'appreciating assets' then remortgage your Property and take out equity [tax free] to do this. We shall look at this in more detail later now that you are thinking about it...

## Summary

Never sell your properties: you have worked very hard to buy them well. Buy at evidenced discount, hold and let your portfolio grow and grow and grow. Take money incrementally tax free.

# Yield [Your ROI]

Throughout this book we've been discussing yield. Yield is the investor's way of gauging a return on a Property investment on a yearly basis. You may well understand yield, and that is great. The definition of yield is hard to pin down, and it seems that people have a wide and varied perception of what it actually is. We like to look at yield in two ways: **gross yield** and **net yield**.

Gross yield is the return on the value of your Property through rent on a yearly basis as a percentage. To give you an example, if you buy a Property worth £100,000 and you get £500 per month rent then your gross yield would be 6% [£500 x 12 = £6000 as a percentage of £100,000].

A nice easy way to calculate this is to multiply rent [500] by 12 and divide that by value [100,000] and you will arrive at a one hundredth decimal figure: In this case 0.06 [or 6%].

Pretty simple. This is a good way to gauge if a Property is worth buying. As we have stated anything around 6% yield or better is good in our game. At the moment, with all the hype and mayhem, and panic, genuine yields of 8% are becoming quite common for us. Yields in reasonable areas where the net yield is still high.

Net yield is something very different. As we see it at Progressive, net yield is the return on the value of your Property through rent on a yearly basis as a percentage, **minus** any additional maintenance and management costs. That is the return minus all the costs associated with your Property.

Here are some great tips for finding those little gem properties with the highest yield:

**Fundamental tip No.10:
Always look for the 'worst' house on the 'best' street.

When you buy a brand new car, let's say a Mercedes again as an example, the difference between a standard model and a fully spec'd up supercharged version can be very significant.

Specifically, a standard Mercedes s-class is around £60,000. However the S-500 is around £100,000 for the same platform with some extra toys and a bigger engine.

In 3 to 5 years nearly all that difference in price disappears, and the S-500 might only be a few thousand pounds more expensive.

Property works the same way. If you have two three bed houses on the same road, both the same size but one has video entry, a plasma TV and oak flooring and is £20,000 more they'll still both rent for the same money give or take £25 because the value of rent achievable is dictated by the 'platform' [location, square footage, no of bedrooms].

The cheaper one offers much better value and a greater yield.

Those who get emotional about Property don't understand this hugely important concept.

Always look for value by buying the 'worst' properties in the areas that will pull the relative value and rentals up. This has a lot to do with land values. It is the land that very often holds the greatest amount of value, and it is the land that can influence the overall price of a property.

On any one street similar plots of similar sizes will hold similar values. This goes some way to explaining why apparently 'worse' properties can achieve similar rents to 'better' properties. You should use this knowledge to your advantage.

Buying Property on good land will always be wise. It's not generally the primary reason we do it, but it will become ever more important. A lot of the stock we are buying nearer the city centre and redevelopment areas is on land that will continue to rise in value.

The one thing we can't get more of in the UK is land, and that keeps demand very high. There's a small chance that over the next 50-100 years your Property could fall down [or at least depreciate significantly], there's almost no chance you'll lose your land. A fallen down or derelict house is worth very little, the land will always be premium.

Net yield can be quite difficult to calculate, and your knowledge of Property type and area and these concepts discussed in this chapter will be invaluable to you. The point about knowing net yield is that you can be allured by high [gross] yielding properties, but in reality most of that return will be spent on maintenance.

As a general rule higher yielding properties over a certain point can end up having a lower net yield than other seemingly less attractive properties [when you do your numbers]. If you have to replace the windows every year or spend money because tenants do not look after your Property, then you can end up with very little at the end of each year. Void periods can also have a big impact [drain] on your yearly return.

Remember that all costs come out of your **profit**. What you are essentially on the look out for [in your area] are those areas where the gross yield is good [properties that are not too expensive, not too big and rent out well] and the maintenance is low [not too grotty, no crime]. You will get to know which areas to avoid at all costs [if the helicopters fly over at night and the rats are running out of town then stay away] and stick to your strategy at the lower end of the market.

You can work out gross yield very quickly and it is a very handy selection tool. Net yield needs a little more research, some experience and a bit of a sixth sense of your area. As long as you keep moving forward with your strategy and follow the rules, you will find those little 'gem' areas. You will become better than 95% of the investors out there and you will make money.

You'll be the 1 in 100.

## Summary

Use gross yield as your gauge for your properties and aim for 6% or better. Understand the difference between gross and net yield. Study your areas as high gross yielding properties can end up with a much lower net yield.

# Interest rates

This comes up time and time again. It already has, just in the few pages of this book.

We have had so many discussions with so many people who are worried about the implication of the rise of interest rates.

First things first: as much as many people remember what happened in the 80's, it is highly unlikely that interest rates are going to keep rising and rising and rising. Most serious commentators believe that the interest rates will level off at about 6% in the current cycle.

The government may want to control house price inflation, but they certainly don't want to trigger a 'crash.' The economy doesn't need it. In order to get a 'crash' [not the tabloid definition] we would normally need to see 2 economic changes rather than, for example, big interest rate rises alone, which would normally mean high rises in unemployment. Neither is likely to happen according to the experts.

So you're still worried? That is not enough of a guarantee for you? You want to be safe? You want to be sure? You were there when the last crash happened?

As you must be aware, you can now fix your interest payments on your mortgage. You can fix them for 3 years. Even 5. Even 10 or 15 if you wish. If you want to be doubly sure that your rate will not increase, then fix your mortgages and you will be covered regardless.

However this isn't always the best option. If the rates fall again you will still be tied in to a higher rate. If you want to access cash through remortgage, but you have a 10 year fixed mortgage that will reduce your options because of high redemption penalties.

However your choice depends on your strategy. It depends on your own personal situation. It is good to know though, don't you think?

Why not consider fixing part of your portfolio. We are currently fixing around one third of our portfolio. We think that this gives us a good safety net if things change. Fix a percentage according to your attitude to risk that you know will look after your retirement. Leave it and let it grow for years. Once you have built that use your subsequent properties to 'play around'. Use them to draw from. Know that if there is a sharp rise that you bought them well and you can still sell them at a profit [not that you ever should, but we're talking peace of mind here]. You still have your golden apple tree.

This brings us to another point. As long as you buy well with your **evidenced discounts**, you know that you have an exit strategy. This is very important, especially if you are risk averse. If you buy well you will always have your get out of jail free card. You know that you can sell and still make profit. You know that you can still sell fast. You know that you are **safe**.

We have mentioned this a few times already; so why not bring it up again: when the interest rates are creeping up and they are putting pressure on people at the lower end of the market, you can profit. Keep yourself ready for this. Stay liquid. Use your equity to get these cheap properties and profit in times where others are unfortunately struggling, and remember to do your best to help them out of debt.

Be stealthy. Be ready to move fast. Only listen to those who know. Rodney down the pub does not have insider knowledge about interest rates.

## Summary

Know that there is opportunity whichever way the market is moving. If interest rates are rising you can profit by buying cheap and helping others out of debt. You can fix your mortgages for peace of mind. Don't panic. Don't sell and don't wait to buy Property. Buy Property and wait.

# Profit in a 'boom' & a 'crash'

Successful investment does not rely on the market.

To become rich, successful, free and independent in the Property game you need to be shrewd. You need to go against the tide sometimes. You need to be flexible. You need to educate yourself; gain experience and knowledge. You need to make a few mistakes and learn from them, and you need to just keep going. Remember **attrition** always wins.

What the market does will not determine your long term outcome. It may have some short term implications which can be both positive and negative [depending on how you look at them] and you will learn from them. Ultimately you are the one in control. The more you stick to the strategy you are building [and follow the rules], the more likely you are to profit.

In the times of a market downturn, skilled investors will make money. Skilled investors will make money regardless of the marketplace. You should look forward to the times when other people have stretched themselves, got it wrong, or been unfortunate, because that is when your superior knowledge will serve you well. You can help them and profit yourself. You can create those 'win-wins'.

Remember whatever the economy, money has to go somewhere. When prices are not moving or going down people will sell. Their flock mentality will kick in. They will panic. They

Rob Moore & Mark Homer

will do what everyone else is doing. They will do what the papers and the guys down the pub tell them. There will be chaos. All hell will break loose. Danger. Danger. Panic. Baa. Baa.

And what will **you** be doing? Sitting. Waiting. Being patient. Not panicking. Sticking to your strategy whilst being flexible. Watching the market. You will be a crouching tiger in the grass. You never see tigers flapping about like lost birds. They stay low. They watch and fixate. They hunt. They pounce.

You will be doing everything the tiger does except you will not kill your prey. You will look after the prey like your very own children. You are the littlest hobo. Until tomorrow, you'll just keep moving on...

Whether you make your money when you buy or whether you make it in growth [or even both], matters not. Always be moving forward. Always be making money.

Things are easier when the market is bull. All of the properties you have amassed will be growing nicely [because you have taken decisive action] and you can roll around in the grass while the other tigers lick your...

Either way the educated investor wins. Either way the educated investor makes money. Knowing that you have a choice, what will it be for you now?

We have written a whole book on this subject, "Make Cash in a Property Market Crash" because there is that much to say on the subject, and that much money to be made now if you're quick:

www.progressiveproperty.co.uk/book2-buy-now.asp

## Summary

Because you are in control you will profit in a 'boom' and a 'crash.' Don't follow the crowd, stick to your strategy. Wait for and take advantage of the many opportunities that will come whatever the market is doing.

Rob Moore & Mark Homer

# Letting & tenancy

Tenant selection can be a minefield.

Perhaps one of the most common fears in Property investment is the prospect of having properties vacant and not being able to rent them out, thus being stuck with mortgage payments on properties.

This is a sensible concern, as void periods consume profits on Property.

We've been studying what types of Property rent out the fastest, the longest and with the least amount of hassle for many years now, through demographics, economics and personal experience.

You have probably realised now what type of Property we like and why. One of the biggest reasons for loving [and making money from] the lower end existing Property market, as opposed to new build, overseas and off plan, is 'rentability.'

We discussed this in section 2, looking at supply and demand and yield in this section.

There is an optimum price point for rentals, and it will vary from area to area. Our optimum price point for rentals is £65,000 - £120,000; specifically studio, 1 & 2 bed flats and 2 & 3 bed houses in 6 specific areas. These areas are 'not best not worst' areas which are affordable to the masses.

When you find these areas with everything you've learned in this book, you'll notice that void periods dramatically reduce to 1 week per year [or under], times to find tenants significantly reduces, duration of tenants staying will increase and the 'pain in the backside' factor will reduce.

We're currently renting out many of our properties within the day after completion and even have a waiting list on many. Our voids are far less than 2 weeks per year and our tenants tend to stay for long periods of time, because of this knowledge.

When it comes to letting out your properties, don't even think about managing your properties yourself. Seriously don't. It will cause you hassle, grief, pain, multiple hernias and coronaries: all to save 10-15% per Property. In the long run it will end up costing you way more; in money and time.

Not everyone will agree with this, and that is fine. Some people have been landlords a long time, and know what they are doing, and have learned to systemise the tasks. It is very difficult without a lot of experience and can tarnish your enjoyment of the investment process. It also goes against all the concepts of leverage that we have been discussing so far in the book.

If you can find a good letting agent then they are worth their weight in gold. It might take a while and you may have to get through a few. However the good ones are worth every penny of the 10-15% they will charge you. But remember they **must** be good. Because you'll be watching over them watching over your properties, it is a good idea to note the following:

**Vet your agents**: always make sure that your agents are working in your best interests. Are they registered with organisations such as NAEA, ARLA, NALS and so on? Type them in Google and you will find them; this is a good place to start in finding an agent, although it will not guarantee that you find a good one.

Check them out. Ask to see details of how they advertise and how [and where] they present the properties that they rent out for you. What papers do they advertise in and how big is the space? How does their website look [do they have one?] and how often is it updated? Compare them with other agents in the area too. And your job has only just started once you have decided on an agent [we recommend trying 3 'against' each other].

You will need to think about the service that you will want them to provide. If you want a 'let only' service, then you will get a basic service that includes the handling of deposits, finding tenants [and not much more].

You really need to be taking their full management service so that you don't have to do any of the inventory work yourself.

Rob Moore & Mark Homer

You don't want to be at the beck and call of your tenants. There are things such as gas and electrical safety checks, cleaning, repairs, maintenance, renewals and so on that you don't really want to be doing. The time that you would be spending on this would be better directed at making serious profit from buying more Property.

Get your letting agent to list their charges, including finding tenants. Check how many times they do an inspection and ask tenants if they have seen the agents when they last came round. Make sure you keep your eye on them, as some have been known to make large amounts of money out of landlords and tenants.

Let your agent know what they need to know [and no more] to get your Property let. When they get complacent their work standards will drop. This is something that we have experienced first hand. They might be a ball of energy to get you, but how do they keep you? If they think they have a monopoly on your business and you get too friendly, things can very quickly go south.

We like our agents to know, in a subtle way, that they are competing with other agents. It keeps them fresh and doing their job. They stay proactive because they want the business and they don't want to lose out to a competitor.

Very often most agents will give you a figure of what they think they can achieve for rent, and then find you someone at £25 or

£50 less than that. We very often take rental figures with a pinch of salt until we have seen figures and tested them ourselves. In some instances we have had to take £50-£100 off what they say they can get, especially when we were new to them, as they were selling themselves to us.

It is a very similar scenario to an estate agent coming round to value your house. If you get a couple round you are not going to use the one that has given you the lowest valuation are you?! How do you think they are going to price your Property?!

It is up to you to set the expectations. If you set the expectation of what you want to achieve, then challenge them to get it [with a view that you will not accept lower], then you may achieve more rent. It can be done, but you must be realistic and aware of how they play their game. You are trying to set the expectations for any future dealings.

We all teach people how to treat us and setting expectations is so important in our game.

It is very important to look for the agents that are prepared to get maximum rent for your property. This is very much a personality thing; some are afraid to ask and would leave your rent at the same figure for 20 years unless you twisted their arm behind their back, pulled their hair and poked out their eyes.

You don't want to use these agents because it tells you a lot about them [much more than just the fact that they won't ask for more rent]. How proactive do you think they will be?

Your cash flow relies on steady incremental increases in the rent. Good letting agents also know this, and want to keep your business, and will do this gradually to keep the tenant happy [better than finding out that the rent has doubled because it has not gone up for 10 years!].

**Vet your tenants**: always make sure your letting agent does a proper credit check on your potential tenant. Any financial grief further down the road will be hugely reduced. Even if you are 'desperate' for a tenant, don't cut corners here. We knew a couple of agents who did not vet their tenants properly and they seemed to attract all of the wrong tenants [and got a reputation for doing so]. A bad tenant can really upset your investments so selecting a good one is vital.

**Always take a deposit**: never let a tenant into your Property without as big a deposit as you can get. It should be at least one month's rent. The more you can get the less likely your tenant is to trash your place and nick your radiators.

**Always have a contract**: this seems so obvious, but isn't always to some investors. An AST agreement should be a pre-requisite for a letting agent, but you should make sure. It is advisable to get your solicitor to look over one the first time you use an agent.

**Make sure you get your monthly statements**: you need to keep a close eye on what is going on. We have had months where our rent has not been paid in. The only way to keep a check is to receive [and read] your monthly statements. It will ensure that your agent knows you are keeping an eye on them and you won't miss anything. Remember that one missed rental payment to you could cause a missed mortgage payment. That could cause a black mark against your credit and hinder further borrowing.

And remember this: *your credit score is your holy grail*. It is your little golden cup. Guard it with your life.

**Encourage your letting agent to systemise everything**: do they have a procedure for everything they do? Are they making sure the gas safety checks are done every year? There is a lot of paperwork around finding and housing tenants. The more disorganised a letting agent is, the less they will get done, and the more problems you will ultimately have. Look for those who systemise and log their procedures and who are attentive to detail.

**Think exit strategy**: Letting is not just about getting a tenant in your Property. Make sure you know in advance that everything is done properly when a tenant may leave.

Don't let the agent release the tenant's deposit until you have inspected the Property yourself. So often have I seen properties not left in the right state afterwards – go round *yourself* and

Rob Moore & Mark Homer

stand firm on the costs to clean and return the Property to the standard that it was when they moved in. You are managing the behaviour of the tenant **and** the agent here. Many people take video evidence of the state of the Property before it was rented which can be used in court. Something to think about.

People often think leaving a Property is like leaving a hotel or taking a rental car back. 'Pick it up clean and take it back dirty without petrol' and the business pays for it. Rented properties don't work like this unless tenants want to pay for cleaning and gardening out of their deposits.

**Be proactive and friendly**: this goes for you and the letting agent. The more proactive you both are, the more you will get done in the shortest possible timeframe. The more your agent looks after your tenant, is likeable, quick and efficient, the more likely they are to both stay and pay your rent on time, every time and treat your place like their own. Despite many myths about tenants, they're human just like us, and respond well to being treated well!

Remember your role in all of this. There is a chain that goes from you to your agent to your tenant. If you bully or complain too often [or even if you are too lenient] then life will be more difficult for you than it should be.

**An opportunity**: letting agents can also be a good source of deals. Make sure you let them know what you want and how you work and open some potential doors. Try to incentivise them to do this. If it is their own business they could invoice you for a finder's fee. This incentivises them and makes them come to you rather than anyone else. Always pay them on exchange of the Property [never before as 1 in 3 Property purchases fall through in the UK and people's attitudes to work can change once they have been paid before all work is done!] and pay them *immediately*. It will only make them more likely to do it again for you. It is amazing what money does to people's passion and productivity!

## Summary

Remember your relationship skills and use other people to leverage the performance of your portfolio. Use a letting agent to find tenants and know what they are supposed to be doing so that you can watch them. They should be friendly, proactive and efficient.

Rob Moore & Mark Homer

# Keep Your costs down

Everything that you spend on your Property portfolio eventually comes out of your profit [or your pocket]. You must know exactly where [and where not] to spend money. Keep a hawks-eye on your spreadsheets and numbers.

Let's get a couple of myths out of the way. Have you watched Property Ladder or any other home renovation programme? Of course, we all have! Perhaps you might enjoy them, which is just fine. Well don't even think about it. These programmes are not aimed at investors. Remember we love Property here in the UK, but we don't seem to be good at making profit from them. Forget the crab candy and the sheep fodder. The strategy is totally different from the one we are using here to make *profit*.

Forget places in the sun that are overseas and inflated by 30% that will rent out for 6 weeks of the year. If you want a holiday home, then spend money you can afford to lose and don't think about it as an investment. Think about it more like a Mercedes 500SL.

Forget huge lavish refurbishments where you spend time, money and put your heart into making a place that you would love to live in for the rest of your life. Again, if you want to do that for your own dream home, then don't think about it as an investment, think about it as a project for you; keep it separate.

Rob Moore & Mark Homer

If you want to **profit** in your investment strategy, then you need to keep the costs as low as you can, and then keep trying to get them lower. Now of course there is a point at which when you do things too cheaply it can end up being far more expensive in the long run; we are not talking about cutting corners here or being a shark.

You will learn the right balance as you go, and it will be specific to your area and the people you use.

**Always get at least 3 quotes for any job**: this is so important. In trades where the trades' people hold the knowledge and skills, it is quite easy for them to pull the wool over your eyes. Boiler quotes are the best example of that. Most of the time you will get told you need a whole new boiler system that will cost you £3,000 when perhaps it is just the ignition that needs fixing.

Be cautious and question **all** costs.

Some of them may try it on if you let them. This is not always the case, but it is best to be sure and get a second opinion, don't you think? Always get 3 quotes and let each supplier/tradesman know that you are doing this. Make them fight for your work.

**You set the expectation**: most people make the mistake of asking for a quote and accepting a price. This is a big mistake. You should be letting any supplier/retailer or tradesman know what you are willing to pay for a job or service and let them meet your price. If they can't; fine. Find someone who can. There will be people out there who want your business.

**Only make basic/light refurbs**: when refurbishing a Property, we are not looking to make a MTV crib footballer's wives home. We are looking to make the Property clean, habitable and neutral so that any person can quickly and happily move in and make their own mark on it. You may like purple carpet, other people may not. You may like floral curtains, mint green wallpaper and brown bathroom suites, other people may not.

Spend your time and budget on kitchens and bathrooms and keep them basic, neutral and cost effective. This is what most people will notice. Carpets should be neutral but dark enough to hide stains; walls should be eggshell white or magnolia to look clean and open. Perhaps spend on light fittings/lampshades or mirrors to make small rooms look bigger, but remember every penny you spend is money out of your profit.

At Progressive we look to keep a full redec [redecoration] under £2,500 and a full refurb [redec plus kitchen and bathroom] under £5,000.

The more you get tradesmen fighting for your work and the more you set the expectation, the more you will be able to get them down to a price that *you* want to pay.

Rob Moore & Mark Homer

**B.O.Q**: always produce a Bill of Quantities [a list of what you expect to be done]. Go through it with the tradesmen and get them to check and sign it to agree. *Do not* pay them all of the money until the job is complete and you have snagged the B.O.Q [check it has been done and make sure you oversee any corrections].

**Remember your relationship skills**: you are managing these processes remember, so think about what you have learned and how good you are with people. Be firm and fair and you will get respect from them and *profit* for your portfolio.

## Summary

Keep your costs down and get 3 quotes for any job relating to your portfolio. This is quite simple really: do not be tempted to spend where you don't need to. Think of it as a business with a tight profit margin and you will succeed. Try not to get too emotionally involved.

# We are all in sales

We are all salespeople. You must be a good salesperson.

We know that many people don't like to think of themselves as salespeople, and we know that many people actually have negative associations around salespeople, but be it good or bad, we really are all salespeople.

We are selling ourselves to others every minute of every day. Every time we debate or argue we are selling someone else the idea that we are right or that we are knowledgeable.

In this book, we are selling to you that we know what we are talking about. We are selling our Property experience and knowledge. If we are not as good salesmen as those new build off-plan Property clubs, then our portfolios are all in trouble!

We are selling all the time. We are selling to our friends, our customers, our colleagues, our boss, our partners and our children. If a child turns to drugs who do you think is the better salesperson, the parent or the drug-dealer?

I know that this is particularly hard for some people to grasp. I [Rob] have coached many people through beliefs about selling themselves and what it actually means.

But it really is pretty simple. If we ever want to borrow money from the bank then we need to sell them on ourselves and our ability to pay them back. If we want to convince someone to sell us their Property for less than it is worth, then we need to be good at selling our trustworthiness and the benefits of using us rather than someone else.

If we want someone to come on a date with us then we need to sell to them that we are good dating material [or tie them up and put them in the boot of your car – no really, *I do not* mean that, it does not work. Mark keeps trying it and I keep trying to tell him there are more subtle methods!].

If you have a preconceived notion about a salesman being the stereotypically suited person who struggles from month to month [mouth] and harasses people, then you need to change that belief now.

The 80's 'Glengarry Glenross' stereotypical salesperson is a thing for museums now; it's not about Eldorado's or steak knives anymore. If you've seen it, you'll know what we mean.

Selling is the process of finding people's needs and giving them what they want. The best salespeople in the Property world are the most ethical, best listening, most conscientious and empathetic people you will meet. They understand totally the desires, beliefs and needs of other people. They know they have great knowledge and offers that people want. They offer value and are relationship experts. They are prepared, diligent, focused on win-win scenarios and great at listening and understanding the world from other people's perspectives.

You are the same, and you will always see sales that way.

## Summary

Being a successful salesperson will lead you to great wealth in your Property portfolio. If we're not convincing people to work with us, to sell their Property to us, to like us; then someone else will.

# Dealmaking, negotiation & estate agents

## Deal making and negotiation

There are certain skills that are essential in attaining long term wealth and success in your Property portfolio. Sales and marketing are essential. A part of any sales or marketing process is being able to negotiate a deal.

We absolutely love this process and the Art in getting better and creating win-win scenarios for the investor and seller [vendor]. This is what will determine your skills as a successful and wealthy Property investor.

Firstly, let us talk about what deal making is not:

Gazumping, ripping people off, lying, pulling out of deals at the 11th hour, reducing your price at the 11th hour, getting one up or skinning people, conning, cheating, bullying or a big ego trip of buying power. This is a sure fire way of ruining your investment career [and losing all of your friends]. We've seen it happen, we've even worked for people just like this in the past, it's not pretty and it doesn't work.

Great dealmanship [I think we made that word up again] will create you far more wealth than a job [or exchanging time for money]. Great deals can return [potentially] a lifetime of passive income [such as negotiating a great Property deal with evidenced discount and a high net yield].

Rob Moore & Mark Homer

If we want to be able to strike great deals then first we must understand negotiation.

**The Art of negotiation**: it is all about coming to an end result that is beneficial to both parties; the vendor and the seller [and not just yourself]. Believe me we tell you this from experience. When we were buying Property in the early days we were heavily focused on how cheap we could get them. Every time we got a deal that seemed so good it wasn't true; it wasn't.

If you cut people too much on price who don't want to be cut, or you leave them having 'won' a negotiation which they 'lost,' they'll very often get buyer's remorse and either change their mind or pull out completely. They can very often end up resenting you and this can tarnish your reputation [your most valuable asset].

The true Art of negotiation is about highlighting perceived benefits to the other party. It is about doing everything you can to help them, making the transaction as easy as possible, and letting them have the last word so that they feel like they have 'won' the negotiation.

**Fundamental tip No.11:
Always leave the seller happy, feeling like they have controlled or won the negotiation [Even if you have just got a 30% discount!].

Rob Moore & Mark Homer

There is a great way of doing this, which involves negotiating in small and non-rounded increments. As you will probably know, most people offer in rounded numbers of £5,000 and £10,000 increments, and very often 'split the difference' in negotiations.

For example; a vendor puts a Property on the market for £120,000. You offer £80,000, they counter with £110,000, you offer £85,000, they come back with £95,000, you offer £90,000 which is begrudgingly accepted.

An experienced negotiator will eat you for breakfast; especially someone who hasn't clearly set their rules yet and is buying on emotion.

The new negotiation might go something like this:

You offer £80,000 on their £120,000 house, they reject your offer and you go back with £85,000. Right away they know that you have more money to spend and that you are negotiating in increments of at least £5,000. This gives them power in the negotiation.

You are now screwed! Admittedly it's not that likely that you will meet a master negotiator with every Property you buy, but you must know this.

At this point you should stop and leave the offer on the table. Most won't, but you will. 1 in 3 deals fall through, so always leave the door open for your offer to be accepted at a later date. We have done deals up to a year after our first original offer.

So the amateur negotiator, having had an increased offer of £85,000 rejected, predictably offers £90,000. The experienced seller, knowing she has a desperate buyer, will not reject this offer, because she may lose the interest of the buyer. She comes down and looks to be 'caving,' but she only reduces her asking price by £3,000 to £117,000. This is not a predictable figure, and could give the impression that this is all the seller could afford.

The buyer, feeling that they are now vested in the negotiation, ups the offer to [you guessed it] £95,000. The seller rejects, but comes back with £116,700, a reduction of £300. This again looks like a specific number, and could quite easily reel in an inexperienced negotiator up to £110,000, through a couple more exchanges.

It is this style of negotiation that you want to employ. Always offer low, because you never know what might be accepted and you have more room to negotiate. Never give away that you have money to burn. Use small and specific increments to hide this. Think about it, if people who you are buying from [and this goes for anything], know you have more money, they're going to want some of it, aren't they?!

In Sun Tzu, the art of war, one of the most fundamental tactics is in never letting anyone know your strategy and situation. This is not war, but the principle is the same.

You need to hold all the power whilst looking like you hold none. Most negotiators like you to know that they are the decision makers. This can also be a mistake, as you have nowhere to go and you could get backed into a corner. That's the great thing about having a business partner; we use each other all the time as the decision maker. We've heard all sorts; 'the wife' is a common [and funny] one. An investing partner or board of investors is also useful because it can preframe that the amount of money available is not down to your decision.

What you are looking to achieve in negotiation is 'situation power.' you are looking to hold the cards, you want them in a position where they need you more than you need them.

Remember you can walk away from any negotiation and leave the door open, so you should always hold situation power. Do not be tempted to get emotional in negotiation. Never tell the seller their expectation of price is unrealistic, even if you know it is. We've done it and seen it done, and it fails all the time. People must get their own lessons, and remember they are selling the most expensive thing they'll ever own, of course they'll want maximum price for it.

'Charm power' is when you have the advantage of being liked. It's very powerful and one of your biggest assets as a negotiator.

Rob Moore & Mark Homer

You'll lose this if you tell someone that they're delusional about the price of their Property. You might be followed by the hounds! Simply restate benefits of buying from you [speed, experience, reliability], offer your help and leave the door open.

These are fundamental points: if you are negotiating a discount, always let the negotiation end on a price that the other party offered so that they feel like they have controlled the deal. Sounds a little silly but if you play your tactics right you will still end on the price you desire. You will also hugely reduce the risk of buyers' remorse or the buyer pulling out of a deal, which can be expensive and annoying.

The one thing that makes the biggest difference in negotiation, and this is so important, is seeing the negotiation from the vendors point of view.

This was such an epiphany for us, in life and in business as well as in Property negotiation. It seems ridiculous, looking back, that we only saw the world through our own eyes, but then that's what we all do, don't we? How can we view life in any other way?!

Everything about your negotiations will be thinking in the mind of the vendor, wearing their skin, in anticipation of what they might think, how they might feel, how they may react and the result they will want to achieve.

Let's be honest, they don't really want to sell their house for 75%

of what it's worth. Think about it. But what they might want is a fast sale, a discreet sale, a hassle free sale, to someone they want to sell to, someone they quite like [no one is ever very likely to sell something to someone they don't like]. Finding those 20-30% BMV deals is all about finding those buyers whose prime motivation for selling is not driven by price. [You'll spot those that are; very often a little stubborn, won't budge on price, often in no hurry, sometimes have an unrealistic perception of the market]. This is totally pivotal, and the more you view, the more agents you use and the more vendors you speak to, the more intuitive you'll become.

You are looking for the people whose prime motivation for selling might be speed or security or discretion. Remember that selling your house can be one of the biggest and most stressful events in your life.

**Fundamental tip No.12:
If you can take away people's pain, you'll go a long way.

Once you've nailed this, everything else will follow gracefully.

**Think co-operation not competition**: Think partnership and long term benefits to building a great relationship. Always remember the following when entering negotiations:

Know the maximum you are prepared to pay and *do not* go over it: don't get the e-Bay bidding syndrome; walk away if the price is not right. There will always be other deals and the chances are at about 30% that you might be re-contacted. Be patient as many deals will come back to you that you didn't expect.

If you are putting enough offers in on properties then you will get some: many vendors wait for months and their expectations change. People's expectation of what they can sell their Property for is nearly always too high, so let the market 'chisel' them down [Mark likes that phrase].

**Know your goal and what you want out of the deal**: this must be planned in advance [remember e-Bay syndrome]. Know your numbers. Find out what they want. Be cool. Be patient. Read into what they are not saying: their posture, body language and what their eyes are telling you.

**Understand the emotions involved in negotiation**: don't wind people up or take the Mickey. Be diligent and educated about the deal. Be flexible: offer other benefits. Be strong and fair and don't give anything away; offer exchange. Let them feel good about the negotiation; it is not a fight or a testosterone kick. Do you know what motivates them? If so use it.

Once you have mastered the Art of negotiation you will be halfway there to being a great dealmaker. Being a great deal maker requires the following traits:

Being a good negotiator!

**Knowing what value and price the Property is worth**: know what the equivalent properties are worth on the same street and of the same type. This is known as 'information power' and is vital in your negotiations. If it is clear to people that you know your stuff then a) you'll command respect and b) no-one will pull the wool over your eyes.

If you don't know your stuff you will end up paying too much. Estate agents can be good at setting your expectations too high [or too low in some cases] so you need to know what the real value of a Property is. What might seem like a good deal in isolation might be expensive when compared to the market.

The biggest mistake that most 'dealmakers' make is that they always state from the outset that they want something cheap or at discount. Do you think that is what the seller wants; to give his Property away for less than he sees it is worth?

**Be opportunistic**. know that you have things, products, services and knowledge that other people need and offer these in return. Be diligent and educated about the deal. Know other people that can help. Be flexible, professional and personable, and always find ways to help the other party.

'100% of the shots you don't take don't go in.' Wayne Gretzky put it very well. Opportunity is the same.

Rob Moore & Mark Homer

When working on negotiation, in our experience in viewing over 10,000 properties, you have more chance in getting a higher percentage discount on a lower priced property.

When using our spreadsheets, the deals are mostly about percentages, with only a few absolute numbers. A 15% discount can give you a no deposit deal, an 18% can mean no cash left in, 20% plus can mean cash out.

We've been keen students of psychology as well as Property and economics, and we have discovered that vendors [sellers] see price in absolute terms, more often than not, rather than percentage terms.

For example, we recently bought a flat for one of our investors for £50,000, which was on the market for £75,000 and worth £70,000 through comparables. This is a massive discount, but in absolute terms is only £20,000 off market value. It is generally as hard for us to get £20,000 off a house that is on the market for £120,000, despite the fact that the percentage discount is much less; only 17% as opposed to 29%!

**Fundamental tip No.13:
Percentage vs. absolute terms. You get bigger percentage discounts on cheaper units.

**Estate agents**

Estate agents could be vital to your negotiation and dealmaking success. They're very often the channel through which you make negotiations, and you will need all of the skills you have just learned in this book to get your desired outcome [low cost, high value properties].

It doesn't matter what you think of estate agents, you need to make these guys your friends. Contrary to what many people believe, most are honest and hard working with a load of knowledge which you can leverage.

It has become ever increasingly 'unfashionable' to buy through estate agents. People have realised that bypassing agents can save time, money and you can negotiate directly with the vendor without a 'gatekeeper.'

There are many ways to find Property, and we run over most of them in this book. Direct marketing is great if done well, but remember that dealing with agents costs you nothing whereas direct marketing can cost significantly.

Despite working on behalf of the vendor, estate agents can be very helpful to you. Their job is to sell properties and meet targets, and for that they need buyers, not just sellers. Their ideal buyer would be fast, efficient, friendly and trustworthy, and someone who is going to buy over and over. Does that sound like someone you know?!

Despite the increase in direct marketing methods, 90% of houses are still sold through estate agents. We get the vast majority of our properties through agents because there is a far lower acquisition cost and there is better leverage in getting someone else [or many agents] doing the groundwork for you.

You can certainly find 'motivated sellers' through direct marketing [leafleting, newspaper ads, the web and so on]. We go into detail about these subjects in our second book: 'Make Cash in a Property Market Crash' where these methods are far more relevant in a static or downward market:

www.progressiveproperty.co.uk/book2-buy-now.asp

Estate agents need good buyers like us, like you, as much as we need them. Not only do they have sales targets, they also have heavy competition from other agents to be proactive so that they don't lose their listings to other agents. This would be a disaster to an estate agent, not so much because of the loss of a couple of grand commission, but more for reasons of competition and reputation. This is vital information, as you'll soon realise where they need you.

Just viewing properties and making offers will build rapport and gain the trust of agents. If you were selling your home through an agent and had not had even a little sniff of a viewing, what would you think of that agent and what would you consider doing? Might you think about listing your Property with another agent? You'd want to feel that something was happening, wouldn't you?

This knowledge is also vital, because you are much more able to help them get what they want. Don't underestimate the power in helping people get what they want. And the beauty of this knowledge is that it aligns perfectly with your goals; view 50, offer on 10, get at least 1. Your low offers may at first start as favours to agents for perceived activity, but some will turn into deals. It's a numbers game.

**Fundamental tip No.14:
The more properties you offer on, the more you will get. The more you offer on at the price you want to pay, the more you will get at the price you want to pay.

If you want 10% BMV deals, you probably won't have to view that many to get one. If you want 30% BMV deals [which are out there] then you'll have to view more and offer lower.

We will get anywhere between 3 and 8 deals that fit into our strict rules on 50 viewings. That's 2 viewings per working day or 10 per working week. We know people who view 10 on a Saturday!

And your numbers will get better too, the more you do.

We have built up a network of estate agents in Peterborough, many of whom have become friends. It is essential to strike up a good rapport with your agents and become someone who they will call ahead of the rest of the pack.

Rob Moore & Mark Homer

It is also very important to build rapport with everyone in the estate agency, not just the boss or decision maker. We see so many people bound in and go straight for the kill, crushing the admin staff in the process. This is a big mistake because a) they could have a good relationship with everyone in the office b) they could be the boss' daughter, spouse or lover and c) they want respect and importance just like everyone else and could be your best route in.

Remember you are a relationship expert. What reason have they got to call you above anyone else?

This takes time and as with any human relationship it is necessary to build trust and understanding. Think of long term relationships and friendships. You will often need to complete on a couple of deals with them over a period of time to really gain their trust as they get 'wide boys' approaching them all of the time looking for 'deals.'

A great way to become close to agents is to go out socially with them; go above what they would expect of you. Perhaps take them out for lunch. Think about what it is that they want. Maybe they have specific interests that you can relate to. Use your creative imagination to add value. Find out what it is that gives the agents their importance and significance. It might be success, power, respect, recognition or simply someone who is nice to them.

Teach them how to treat you and be clear about what you want. Give them a *specific* set of criteria by which to look for Property for you. This saves time, makes them realise that you are serious, and you will end up getting offered more of what you want.

The more specific you are with your buying criteria, the more likely you are to get what you want. It sounds ridiculously obvious, but if you're not, you'll end up being offered what the estate agents want to sell you, and you'll either have to keep rejecting them to the point where they stop offering to you because they don't think you'll buy, or you'll end up offering on stuff you don't want [that's not within your rules] because you'll feel you have to.

Remember this is your game, you set your rules, and it is down to you to communicate this with agents and teach them how to treat you and what to bring you.

Once you have viewed a Property get back to them immediately with your thoughts and an offer if necessary. This will again let them understand in a more specific way what you are looking for and will keep you in their mind for when the next deal comes along.

*Mindspace* is a big thing when dealing with anyone, not just estate agents. When selling or buying anything, or even just trying to get a girl on a date [we should know we have tried often enough!] you need to "occupy a space" in another person's mind. The more times the potential buyer [or date] hears from or about you, the more likely they are to go for what you are selling [very often yourself]. This is what big brands understand. Get into their unconscious mind. That's right. Just where you want to be.

Always be honest with them. If you don't want a Property tell them immediately and why. If you do, try to gauge where the vendor is [what is their expectation?] on price. The agent is likely to know this, so if you get on the right side of them they are likely to tell you.

Although they can't tell you exactly what offers they have had for a Property they will be able to give you a good idea. This can be really helpful for you [for obvious reasons].

You may not get the Property the first time as the vendor's expectations may be too high in terms of price. It may work later for the vendor though, and you may get the Property for a reduced amount, when the market has reduced their expectation.

*Never but never* pull out of deals - this is *so* important. You will shatter any trust you have with the agent and make it very unlikely that they will give you any deals again.

The whole idea of them coming to you with Property is that you are a fast purchaser who is not in a chain. You guarantee to buy and they will have a hassle free sale [and earn their commission quickly].

They can then 'sell' this to the owner of the Property who actually needs a purchaser like **you**. It gives you advantage over other buyers in their eyes. They may be in financial difficulty and facing repossession of their home, which you will stop if you purchase their home [quickly]. They may be going through a divorce or the Property may be part of an estate of a deceased person and the executors may be trying to sell it quickly to pay the inheritance tax.

The point is that all of these situations require a fast guaranteed sale and in return these vendors [or sellers] are willing to accept a reduced below market value [BMV] price for the Property. In these circumstances price is **not** the most critical factor. The agent is looking for a purchaser like **you** to take the Property; someone who can offer a sure, fast sale.

**Fundamental tip No.15:
To get great BMV Property, you need to find vendors whose primary motivation for selling is **not** price.

The second you show them that you won't provide this is the second that the estate agents will stop offering you deals.

So even if you realise that you have paid more than you wanted to, or that the refurbishment work may cost more than you thought, go through with the sale. It will cost you a lot less in the long run. Agents [like everyone] talk, this is what they do for a living, and you want them to be talking about you in the right way: positive mindspace.

You may also find that you are competing with the owner/manager of an estate agency for deals, as they are in a perfect position to take advantage of them. They see deals everyday because that is what they do. Try to be reasonable and not to get into bidding wars with owners of estate agents, or anyone else over a Property, as you will annoy them [and end up paying too much]. It is their patch, and that is the way they see it. You are diplomatic and reasonable. Your reputation is everything.

It is a good idea to try and get on the right side of the owner or manager if they are taking deals themselves. I [Mark] can think of one particular owner of an estate agency in our town who has bid on the same properties as myself. This has happened for sale both through his agency and through others. This has not always created a great situation and I wish I had managed to form a relationship with him beforehand.

Buying and selling houses, whilst popular on TV, costs a lot more than people think. On average it costs about 10% of the sale price to buy, pay the mortgage and sell a Property in 6 months. On top of this you a have the renovation costs, your time and tax. We try to steer clear of doing this. We are not in the game of sinking money.

# Summary

Be great at dealmaking and negotiation and you will attract wealth in your ever growing portfolio. Always be thinking in terms of the other person's wants and needs and aim to present 'win-win' negotiations.

# Understand marketing

Marketing is how we get to communicate with the world.

If we don't know how to tell people about what we do [and more importantly how we can help them] then no-one will ever know, will they? It sounds so obvious, but most people don't really understand how to market themselves, their products, their brand or their offers.

When I [Rob] used to paint, in my harder days as an artist, I totally knew nothing about marketing, so little that's it's almost embarrassing. I couldn't sell because I was scared, no one knew about my work other than through recommendation, and the talent that I had was totally wasted and slowly driving me insane because I couldn't get any of my work seen.

Now this is not a marketing manual but why don't we look at the most important things that you should know regarding marketing to attain desirable and profitable properties for your portfolio. Is that ok with you?

In building your portfolio and finding the deals that you want, you need to think of marketing as a two way process:

1. How you market yourself.
2. How you appeal to the needs of others.

1. How you conduct yourself, your image, your brand [because

everything that says anything about you is your brand] is of vital importance.

Are you organised, friendly, efficient, consistent and trustworthy? If you are, sellers, agents and contacts will be happy to do business with you. They may even go above what's expected of them and surprise you because of how you have treated them.

Just look at how Richard Branson manages to instil such brand values within his organisation. He gets passionate people [not monkeys] working for peanuts. He conducts himself in such a way [passionate, committed, fun-loving] and people are attracted to that.

**Warning**: Wasting people's time, being a big shot, trying to steal deals, being inconsistent and not telling the truth [traits we have seen all too often in the Property industry] will seriously damage your long term wealth.

2. How to appeal to the needs of other people.

We are not really talking about the traditional definition here; something like:

'The total of activities involved in the transfer of goods from the producer or seller to the consumer or buyer, including advertising, shipping, storing, and selling.'

Thanks to dictionary.com, though it doesn't really help us to make profit in Property. Every great marketer we've studied will say that marketing is about how you deliver a message that triggers a desired decision in someone's mind. It's about cutting through the noise, getting positive mindspace and turning that into your desired action.

That could be a buying decision [action] or a selling decision [action]. What is important is that you understand the ways in which you communicate, and how they can trigger [or turn off] the outcomes you desire. If you can occupy space in the mind of someone you want to make a buying decision in a positive way, you have nailed marketing.

At Progressive we use many forms of marketing, and you may well have been exposed to one or more of these media [if so then Rob is doing his job – good boy!]. These include direct mail, e-mail marketing, joint ventures, affiliate marketing, websites and Google Adwords [PPC], viral marketing, commission based incentives, word of mouth referrals and so on.

There is so much marketing 'noise' nowadays, how can you cut through it all and leave a lasting impression. Do you even believe that you can?

For the purposes of you finding Property that will make you money, we think that the ones you should concentrate on are internet [website] marketing, leafleting [direct mail], using estate agents and publications [newspapers], and word of mouth.

**Website [internet] marketing**: again, this is a whole new book here [of which Rob has read a few]. If you want some more detail drop Rob an e mail:

robmoore@progressiveproperty.co.uk

We also have some good ones on our reading list:

www.progressiveproperty.co.uk/readinglist.asp

One thing I will tell you: if you can master marketing on the internet you will have the ability to earn on a *massive scale* for the rest of your life. And I don't just mean in Property; I mean anywhere.

Things in internet marketing have changed forever. Since Google Adwords [and other paid CPC/PPC platforms] have come about, you can reach millions of potential buyers [or sellers] in minutes. It's absolutely phenomenal. It's the new eBay. I have acquired investors for Progressive that commit to us for 6 years and pay large sums of money for next to nothing. I'm talking less than ten pence.

One particular keyword ad cost us 42 pence and gave us a 65,476% return on investment. Another ad cost us 9 pence and gave us a 305,556% return [in about 2 weeks]. We have so many other examples just like that. Beat that anywhere and I'll eat a copy of this book.

We are as much marketers as we are Property investors. If you want to make big money on a regular basis, you might want to think of yourself in the same way now. Most of you reading this book are doing so because of marketing on the internet.

Yes it excites me. You darn tootin' it does! It does more than excite me, it's the technological form of Viagra [not that I have tried Viagra. Cough].

Things are changing now too, and with change comes massive opportunity. We have now moved to web 2.0, which includes social networking and bookmarking, video and audio, Facebook and YouTube, webinars and other methods of marketing that offer opportunity to reach more and more people. We've said it enough times but we'll say it again, with all of this rapid change comes your chance to get in at the early stage and make money before anyone else.

OK, so here are the fundamental things in marketing that you must remember:

**Trust**: people will only buy from or sell to people they trust. Remember that in some instances you are buying Property from people under very sensitive circumstances, so they absolutely must be able to trust you.

There are enough sharks out there, so be the gentle and chirpy dolphin and genuinely desire to help others, and you will find all the 20%+ deals you want. This is relevant in all forms of marketing: your website, your leaflets and your dealings with estate agents.

And the same principles always apply in person, in print or on screen.

There is a real science to this that we find fascinating. Putting a woman's name instead of a man's name on a leaflet to receive a call increases conversion. The difference between a mobile number, and 0845 number and an 0800 number can be huge. Putting a headline in quotation marks does too. Black copy on a white background with a red headline generally converts the best. Pictures increase conversion, guarantees and risk reversals increase conversion.

Testimonials and how others have benefitted increases conversion.

And even more interestingly is that everything you read and study about that makes people make buying decisions differs from market to market and the only one thing you can do to make sure is test them all yourself.

**Understanding your target market**: This is vital. Talking to 16 year olds about knitting and bingo, or 70 year olds about adding big blowing exhausts and air filters to their 'B-reg' Nova is not going to interest them in the slightest. When marketing and communicating with people to get them to make a buying or selling decision based on your words alone, you must absolutely know who you are talking to. This is called demographics.

There is one very easy and often overlooked way of doing this effectively: put yourself in their shoes, in their skin, see the world through their eyes and you'll understand how to make connections with your market.

Even easier still: ask them!

**WIFM?** What's in it for me? This is all that people are interested in: period. They don't care about you [honestly, they don't]; they just care about how you can help them [in the case of buying repossessions, for example] or how your product or service can benefit them.

The more you understand the people you are communicating to; their behaviours, decisions, interests, places they go, films they like; seriously the more you know, the more you can communicate to their model of the world: *rapport*.

We all like to be around, buy from and sell to people we like and have common interests with. This is so important in marketing.

**Communication**: Whether it is how you speak to an estate agent or how you write your website/leaflets, how you communicate is paramount. Understanding your market is not enough. You need to know how to communicate with them effectively so that they get it; so that you trigger that desired *decision*.

The Art of the written word is simple. Be clear, be concise. Use plain and simple English that everyone can understand [no one likes a smart-ass self professed Guru do they?]. Talk in terms of other people's interests [all the way back from Dale Carnegie] and get them saying **Yes Yes**. Think **WIFM** and benefits.

**Testing and measuring**: I think this is the most important aspect to marketing, and one that most people overlook completely. Don't shortcut this.

The best marketers in the Property world; the ones who get consistent deals of 15%+ evidenced discount do so because they do not give up [*attrition* always wins] and because, in their continual search, they are always looking to improve.

Anthony Robbins promotes constant and never ending improvement. Amen. But we need to actually be able to measure our improvement, otherwise how do we know that we are actually getting anywhere?

Most people guess.

These are the people who don't make any money, and that is not why you are here. Test everything you do. How many calls do you get per 1000 leaflets delivered? How many deals do you get per visitor[s] to your site? How many deals do you get per viewing?

How many deals do you get per converted lead from Google and at what cost? How much time you spend to generate income?

We know people [and Property clubs] that are actually spending more to get their deals than the deal actually offers, and they don't even know it! We are not here to lose money are we? Marketing costs can spiral out of control if not kept an eye on.

Know your numbers and test all of your marketing. Use different phone numbers on leaflets. Use Google Analytics on your website. Split test ads on Google Adwords to keep improving them. Split test ads in print media. You should always AB test [split test] one thing at a time [headline, text font, pictures etc] and continually try to beat your best performing ad.

Successful advertising marketers like Claude Hopkins have been doing it way back since the late 1800's.

I [Mark] keep a notebook of every Property I have viewed, and we know that for every 8 properties we view we get one Property that works at the figures we want, as per our buying analyser. From that we know our numbers and can look to get better at sourcing so that we are buying one in 6, for example.

Rob Moore & Mark Homer

**Know that there is a cost to all marketing**: many people may tell you that joint venturing or other forms of marketing have zero cost. This is wrong. Everything in life comes at a cost, and it is important that you know what your cost is.

How much time out of your life does your marketing take? Is that time replacing other tasks that make you money or give you enjoyment? Are you delivering all of those leaflets yourself? Are you paying someone else to do it [who might deliver 30 then throw the other 9,970 in a skip?]. Property is a very time intensive career and that needs to be measured so that you can get the right balance for you [or get someone else to do it for you so that you can take the benefits without the time cost]. Your website marketing may cost 10 times as much as your leaflet marketing. I don't know. It will be up to you to test, but don't you think that is useful information for you to have?

Maybe you should spend more time with agents and gaining their trust to leverage them. You will know through testing. Remember that cost is not just about money. It can be time; it can be happiness or it can be freedom.

# Summary

Think **WIFM** [what's in it for me] and benefits to others when marketing to them. The more rapport you have with any contact or vendor, the more likely you are to get your desired outcome. Understand the many channels to market and test them all against each other so that you know that you are constantly improving.

Rob Moore & Mark Homer

# Become an expert

Only listen to those who **really know** and have done what it is that you want to do.

As we have discussed earlier, many people will be happy to give you their opinion about all manner of things. This is just fine; we are all entitled to that, and we think it is good to be open minded.

However the only way we are going to become an expert is to listen to the experts [rather than newspapers and pub talk] and then physically go out and get the necessary experience.

Actively seek out people with a portfolio of 20+ properties or more and see how you can help them, so that in turn you can learn from them. Find out what kind of properties they are buying and their strategy. Are they diligent? Do they focus in a particular area and on a particular Property type?

In the NLP world [an interesting place] there is much talk about modelling. And we're not talking about clay or Plasticine or trains or aeroplanes here: modelling in the sense of studying how something and someone works [and becomes an expert] and then replicating their strategy [or at least the things that work in that strategy].

**Success and wealth leave tracks**. There are learned systems, strategies, mindsets and behaviours that lead to great wealth.

Rob Moore & Mark Homer

Your mission: find them and replicate them. Then turn that knowledge into cash.

That is where most people fall down; monetisation. The get most of the way towards a goal but can't make the last [and most important] step.

The experts make the most money. The people who have been doing what they do and have become great at it make the most money. They have the most value and other people want that. It's almost insane to get 95% of the way there and not make that final step.

I [Rob and Mark!] used to be too proud in my youth to learn from those who were good. I was always either a tad jealous or thought they were just plain lucky. The best thing I ever did was grow out of my ego. Don't ever think that you know it all; we can all learn so much from each other if we just ask, listen and stay open minded. Remember, from what we have discussed earlier, that many people get their sense of importance from talking, being listened to, telling stories or educating others. We all have unique talents; it's good to listen to people, and amazing what we can find out.

We now regularly pay £1,000's per session for people who are experts in their respective fields and can teach us things that will give us huge ROI's.

Wealthy and successful Property investors are so for a reason. Most of the time it is not down to luck. Most of the time you can find out their strategies, and most of the time they will be happy to share their knowledge with you.

Make it a life long mission of yours to seek out those who have what you want and to learn from them. Read books about wealthy and successful people you admire. Subscribe to their newsletters and read their blog entries. Hunt them down and buy them lunch. Take them out and ask them how they did it. Sleep with them if you have to [Ha!]. Believe me they'll be happy to share their stories with you.

Learn from their mistakes as well as their successes. Save yourself years of time, energy, trial and error. Become the one who is writing the book and teaching other people how to do it.

Learn the walk of the rich and successful [it works apparently].

Try and get as much coverage for what you are doing as you can. As you build your portfolio contact editors of relevant local and Property publications and let them know what you are up to. If you publish on a website contact them with your entries. They will not always respond to you right away, but just keep letting everyone know of your successes and they will want a piece of you.

Knowledge and action are power. Do you have contacts that can help you reach more people? Do you have a story to tell that radio or TV might be interested in? We all have something to tell.

Can you mentor other people and teach them what you know. We know that you are an expert in one area, we all are uniquely talented. Transfer what worked in that strategy to your Property portfolio [remember transmutation?].

Success leaves tracks. Use other people successes and expertise to help you to become a wealthy and successful Property investor.

## Summary

Become an expert in Property and you will be successful. Your strategy will work for you and others will want to learn from you. Alternatively find an expert and leverage their skills and experience.

# Capital gains & IHT [and how to pay less tax]

There are many books that have been written on this subject, and believe us; it can be a bit of a minefield. It is not our intention to send you into oblivion with legalities here, but to try to simplify the best ways to avoid paying unnecessary tax.

The Laws are changing all of the time and at any budget the thresholds can be changed. We advise getting a good accountant who specialises in this area, who is proactive and perhaps has a bit of an entrepreneurial streak; someone who has your best interests in mind and knows your goals.

Just to give you a brief overview of tax around Property, you can be taxed in 4 main ways: stamp duty, capital gains, income tax and inheritance tax.

**Stamp duty**: when you buy a Property you will have to pay stamp. If you notice throughout this book, we mention that we are buying Property under £125,000; well that is because we are saving 1% stamp.

Stamp duty is currently set out as follows:
Up to £125,000: 0%
£125,001 - £250,000: 1%
£250,001 - £500,000: 3%
£500,000+ 4%

This is important information for your strategy. You should be able to negotiate prices around the stamp duty thresholds. Very often little 'vacuums' in the market are caused around this. You may get a Property that is really worth £130,000 - £135,000 for £125,000 because of the 'sticking point' around the stamp duty threshold.

A sharp Property investor will always be on the look out for these 'vacuums.'

Conversely, if you don't stick to the strategy and you buy a Property for say, £255,000, it will actually cost you £262,750. That is an additional £7,650 you have paid in tax. That could be nearly a year's growth [profit] on a small Property down the swanny!

**Income tax**: this is not really relevant to this strategy. You will pay tax on a self assessment basis, in your tax bracket, on any income received through rent.

If you never sell, you'll never pay tax.

As a side note: you can claim certain expenses against your tax, as you can a business, and landlords are given incentives [tax relief] because the government can't keep up with demand. The government want more investors [landlords] to help them house people in our society, especially first time buyers who are finding it ever more difficult to get on the housing ladder. As the numbers of council houses are reducing the amount DSS claimants needing rental property are soaring.

Rob Moore & Mark Homer

This is another reason why we use the remortgage capital growth strategy. If we run our portfolios at cash-flow even or there-abouts, there is no income tax to be paid.

A relevant point to note here is your loss carried forward. If you register a loss on your income tax for the year, you can carry that forward and it can be offset against the future years that you may make profit. Many of the properties that you buy currently, even if bought well, may make a small loss, especially if you claim your full relief [letting agents' fees, legal and professional fees, ground rents and insurances, cleaning, travel, wear and tear and so on].

Yes we are getting more technical here, but if we thought that you weren't ready for it, we would have included it in our 2nd book!

**Capital gains tax**: can be a stinger. The capital gains process is complicated and depends on your income [and what you can take as relief], but as a general indication on a portfolio you will be paying up to 40% of your gain that you make for the majority of that gain [profit].

We shall make the assumption that your investment properties were not bought before April 1998, when the tax was worked out on an 'indexation' basis: boring, complicated and somewhat irrelevant. You will be buying most, if not all of them, in the future.

Rob Moore & Mark Homer

The rules have since changed to become 'taper relief.' Incidentally, they'll probably change again by the time you re-read this book!

Taper relief works on any Property that is classed as a 'non-business asset;' applicable to any Property after your primary residence [home]. It is a tax 'relief' where the longer you hold your asset, the less capital gains tax you pay:

Property held less than 3 years: 0
Property held 3 – 4 years: 5%
Property held 4 – 5 years: 10%
Property held 5 – 6 years: 15%
Property held 6 – 7 years: 20%
Property held 7 – 8 years: 25%
Property held 8 – 9 years: 30%
Property held 9 – 10 years: 35%
Property held 10 years+: 40%

Some figures to [hopefully] make sense of it all:

You bought a Property 11 years ago for £50,000 [inc. costs]. That Property is now worth £180,000 and you want to sell it. The pre-tapered gain is £130,000 [new value – old value] multiplied by 40%: £52,000

Your taxable gain therefore is £130,000 - £52,000 = £68,000

Follow so far? Well that's not all. The government give us a small allowance each year called an annual exemption, which goes up with inflation, and is currently £9,200.

If you buy a Property in joint names [as we do for many of ours] you can double that exemption.

That is £68,000 - £9,200. This leaves £58,800.
Now if you are a higher rate tax payer you will have a tax bill of 40% of £58,800, which is £23,520.

Multiply that by a few [all of your future investment properties] and you have a fairly hefty tax bill on your hands.

So did all of that confuse the hell out of you? If not then you should be working for the Inland Revenue! However, if that sends you into a bit of a spin then don't worry. The whole point of this is that you can avoid all of the messing around, calculating and analysing by holding your properties and never selling them!

You should know this by now! And at least you can't say that we didn't tell you.

Now we don't know about you, but we want to do as much as we can to reduce our tax bill. The simplest way in Property terms is, and we'll say it again: to **never sell your Property**.

Rob Moore & Mark Homer

**Fundamental tip No.16:
Never ever sell a good, solid investment Property.

We recommend that you forget trying to buy Property in companies, anything 'off-shore' or buying Property in other people's names [and so on] for the purposes of saving tax. It might save you a little tax in the long run, but it will require expertise, can end up costing and taking up a lot of your time, and may give you a long term headache.

If you hold your properties and access your gains through remortgage, then you are effectively accessing your gain by borrowing it against the value of your Property. You do not have to pay tax against a loan [mortgage]. The great thing about this system is that most people remortgage every three years or so anyway and actually never pay off their mortgage. They can apply this strategy without changing anything they do. All we need to do is buy more Property and compound the gains and keep accessing them this way.

This enables you to access your money incrementally rather than having to wait 25 years for it. This also saves you shed loads of tax! In addition, this reduces your inheritance tax bill because you have less profit in your asset when it comes time to pass it on.

**Inheritance tax:** can be just as nasty. The more assets you own when it comes to passing them on, the more tax the recipients will have to pay. Using the same strategy, if you have been borrowing and taking equity from your portfolio as you earn it, your IHT bill will be greatly reduced.

If your portfolio has grown to £5million and throughout your life you have used the equity to live, buy more assets and enjoy your life, then your children or other recipients will have a much reduced tax bill.

Some figures for you:

Traditional thinking: own one Property outright. Bought for £50,000 in 1985, worth £800,000 in 2025 [generic example based on historical growth]. Mortgage fully paid off:

Initial taxable profit: £750,000.

*Progressive thinking*: own 11 properties using equity from your first home. Total portfolio value in 2025: £4million [conservative estimate of only 5% growth]:

Taxable equity of 15%: £600,000.

To see figures that to show how much leverage you can obtain from the remortgage of *just one* Property, see page 385

Using traditional thinking, you have paid off your own Property by 2025. Your asset has grown to £800,000 in 40 years and you have not remortgaged it. You have not been able to use, invest, spend or enjoy any of that money and your next of kin are lumbered with a big tax bill.

Using **Progressive thinking,** you have used equity in your own home to buy more Property. Perhaps you bought the next 10 from that one remortgage or you kept remortgaging over the next 20 years and re-investing. You have taken your money as your Property has grown in value and you have enjoyed at least **£1.25milllion** in that time. Your asset base only has equity in it of £600,000 [less than with traditional thinking] and the tax bill you are leaving is less on a considerably larger asset base.

In all the years of investing, studying, testing, trailblazing and meeting the richest investors, we have not yet found a better strategy than this.

## Summary

Never sell your properties. Remortgage and take your cash tax free incrementally over your life to reduce your capital gains and IHT bills considerably.

# Section 5:  What Are You Going to Do Now?

Rob Moore & Mark Homer

A quick breath: that's nearly all the information you need. Now it's time to turn your knowledge into cash [only if that is Ok with you of course]...

## Conscious vs. unconscious

So now you have all the tools, you really do.

But of course you know that this is not the end of the road. The rest is up to you and the action you take from here on.

I hope that we will talk in the future and you will be telling us your stories of action and success, and hopefully some of those will be down to what you have read here in this book.

**Fundamental tip No.17:
The difference between the experts and the beginners is what they know *unconsciously*.

When tiger Woods hits a ball 350 yards do you think he is thinking consciously about the wind and the length of the grass and the molecules in the air and the trajectory of the ground and the way his hips move in relation to his legs and how all of his fingers are interlinked on his grip and his shoulder turn?

When Mariah Carey sings do you think she is conscious of reading the lyrics and reading the musical notes and the tension in her larynx and how much air is in her lungs and if her dress is too tight and if her face looks funny when she hits the high notes?

It's just like the secrets in this book. We think you knew that they weren't secrets really, because secrets are just things that

Rob Moore & Mark Homer

successful people know that not so successful don't know yet. But everything you didn't already know was a secret, and now everything is out in the open.

These 44 'secrets' [to the others, not to us] have become more and more unconscious for us. It was actually quite hard to write this book and get all of this information articulated for you, because most of it just comes to us like riding a bike; we do it naturally without always consciously knowing what we are doing or how we are doing it.

And this is the key to becoming an expert. This is the key to becoming successful, wealthy, free and happy.

It is turning all the things in this book that you will need to do consciously at first into unconscious actions. It is through reading the book again. It is through taking action and making the odd mistake. It is through asking questions and discovering new answers. It is through learning. It is through listening and observing. It is through growing and achieving.

If there is one secret that is more important than the rest, then it could well be this.

# 5 The magic number

So what is the magic number? Well yes, we have told you it is 5, but what does that mean?

In our buying experience, and having met and modelled some of the most successful Property investors, we have calculated that 5 properties in your portfolio is the magic number to be able to comfortably live without the need for work.

In a nutshell: your financial independence, your security and a passive income that you should be able to live on for the rest of your life [and beyond].

It is the number of properties that will allow you [picture this] holidays in the sun every year, shopping trips and relaxing spa sessions, Callaway Golf clubs and long weekends free to use them to shoot under par scores, convertible Mercedes' ski trips and Rolex watches, Chloe handbags and anything else that you could imagine that you would love to have and not have to work for.

Of course we all have different expectations of what our finances and future should look like. We have calculated that twice the average London wage, tax free, per year, would suit and benefit most people nicely. It does for our clients and investors, and it could for you.

Rob Moore & Mark Homer

And if you want more? Just buy more Property using the same strategy. Replicate success.

How about we do some maths? To buy 5 properties using the high street strategy is going to cost around £150,000 upwards. This is very dependent on your area, and as you know, we are buying properties at the moment under the stamp duty threshold.

That is £25,000+ per Property and includes deposits, refurb costs, fees and a little contingency. If you buy one a year in 5 years you might have 5 investment properties.

We shall talk about what you will earn in a minute. If you have been absorbing the content of this book you will know that effectively using the knowledge here, you can actually use one set of deposits/fees/refurb costs/contingency to buy those 5 properties. That's one set of costs for 5 properties, not 1 Property. Most people will never ever have a clue how to do this. Most people will never ever believe it can be done; because most people live in the world of 'I don't know what I don't know so it can't be done.'

You buy one Property per year [you get your desired Property type in a desired area at an evidenced discount of 15% or more]. You put your 'pot' [£25,000+] in and then you add value to your Property. You remortgage and get your 'pot' back out.

Do this for 5 years at a nice steady pace and there you have it: 5 properties. That is all from the cost of one 'pot' which has come back to you and can either go back in the bank or continue to buy you more Property [why would you stop?!].

And now for the maths: If you are buying, as suggested, at around £105,000, then you should be able to get these properties valued up to around £125,000 [buy cheap, add value, revalue].

Your 5 properties will be worth around **£850,306** [including incremental growth] at the end of year 6. See exact figures on page 387

Please note: remember that the values of the Property you buy will depend on your area, and we are using examples of the types of properties we buy in Peterborough.

You might be thinking that £125,000 x 5 is not £850,306, and you would be right. Remember the market should be growing year on year, so your relative properties will be worth more year on year. We use growth figures of 8% for our calculations, well below the actual current and historical average of 11.74 % since 1952. We like to be safe.

If you want to be extra cautious, use 5% and bear in mind that properties went up 1.1% in July 2007 alone. Your portfolio would still be up at over £750,000. See page 387

Rob Moore & Mark Homer

Since updating this book to its second edition, the market has changed. No surprises there, it will continue to do so. For a specific definition of an asset and how to buy to make profit in this very interesting time [full of huge opportunity for the few who really want it], log on to the address below:

www.progressiveproperty.co.uk/book2-buy-now.asp

Your portfolio at year 5 is worth **£850,306**. That will have equity of around **£226,725** [your mortgages taken from your total portfolio value]. See page 385.

Growing at 8% per year you will earn £73,466 in your first year of apple collecting. If you want to be extra safe then let's call it 5%: you will be earning £45,917 per year [tax free].

The average London wage is around £35,000 currently. If we multiply that by two and take off the tax and national insurance, that works at around £40,000 net earnings [less than your portfolio at a conservative 5% that will earn for you while you sleep!].

There we go. Perhaps we are making it sound too simple? We hope so, because it really is. Why pay tax? Why work in a job you hate? Why work at all if you don't want to?

We have experienced this same effect, but with a much larger portfolio and much higher growth figures. Investors who made hay in the late 90's and early 2000's would have experienced even more growth and tax free earnings.

## Summary

You only need 5 investment properties to be financially secure and independent for life. You can probably access enough money from the equity in your house to build that portfolio now and release money incrementally, tax free, through remortgage.

Rob Moore & Mark Homer

# Time: Your most precious commodity

Money- we can get back. Trust, love, Property – we can get back. Revenge – we can get back. Muscle and fitness, even good looks [with the aid of cosmetics] – we can get back.

You know where we are going with this one, don't you? The one thing in life that we can't get back is *time*. It is the one thing that is most valuable to us. The one thing we really shouldn't waste. The one thing we should treat so preciously.

We believe that you should be so selective in how you use your time. *Do things you love.* Do things that build you a future. Do things that make you money. Do things that build your Property portfolio and your future. Do things that help others.

Don't waste your time with anything else. Don't waste your time doing things you don't want to do if you don't have to.
Now of course there are things we all do that we don't particularly like, and we have the choice as to whether we do it or not.

We don't particularly like paying speeding fines, parking tickets, doing changes of address and so on [on our portfolio, it's a real pain in the ass], but unless we're going to get someone else to do that kind of stuff for us [which we recommend], then we either choose to get on with it or leave it.

Rob Moore & Mark Homer

It is all about **choice**. What do you want to do with your time? Where you put your time will absolutely dictate your results so think very carefully about this one. Be selective. Be ruthless. Throughout the time that we've been building our portfolio and businesses, we have always strived to become more efficient. We have always looked at how we can get better and better and do things quicker. We have reduced the amount of properties we look at in order to get a deal. We have built systems to make all of our buying and investor processes fast and efficient, and we have improved the quality of our own work immeasurably; focusing on our IGT's [Income Generating Tasks].

You can outsource and sub-contract, you can leverage. You can choose that you are only going to do what you love, what you want, and what makes you money, and the rest can be delegated. We can get anything back but time and we all have a very finite amount of it.

One of the reasons we wrote this book was because we would have hated to take to the grave the things we have learned; what a waste that would be.

We think the point here is that the more efficient you become in everything you do, the more you can save yourself precious time to do the things that you love the most.

Maybe that might be to find more of those deals, maybe to spend time with loved ones, or whatever it is that you choose.

Rob Moore & Mark Homer

And that is the most important thing. The more you respect time as precious and become super-efficient, the more time you will have, and the better your life will be.

## Summary

Use your time wisely because it flies by. Don't waste a minute. Make your decisions quickly; you have the information you need to go out and make it happen for you right now.

Rob Moore & Mark Homer

# Decide on Your strategy

Unfortunately, we know that 90% of people who read this book will now go and do nothing. Statistically the sofa, the Playstation 2, the Pub, the bingo hall and the bookies are all far more appealing than getting up, going out and making cash! Now we know that is not you, but that fact still remains.

Knowing that you want to do something about it; you have 2 choices [you have dismissed the watch TV and do nothing strategy, haven't you?]:

**Strategy 1**: Take everything that you have learned here and go out and get your 5 properties. Then buy 5 more and 5 more and keep going as long as you desire. You really can do it. It won't always be easy, but nothing that ever meant anything was. It will take time, effort, dedication, money and hard work; but you really can do it.

It can be done part time to start with, but once you get to that magic number it will become a full time career, so you need to think about that and if you want it to be that way for you.

If you follow the principles and 'secret' tips in this book, and its sister book "Make Cash in a Property Market Crash," and if you use them as a manual then you will succeed; guaranteed. So many people before you have done exactly that using exactly the same tools and tricks, and most of them started from a similar position as you, if not further back.

Rob started with £30,000 worth of debt and over £20,000 per year in interest payments on loans and credit cards. Mark started with a very basic salary and a very small amount of business knowledge.

You know you can raise finance as we have discussed earlier, no matter where you are in your life, and no matter what your financial position. You can get started right away by setting your strategy and making it happen.

You don't need us. You can become a full-time Property investor and you can make whatever wealth you want to make and beyond. Please just make sure you tell us all about your successes, we would love to know and be a part of it in some way.

**Strategy 2**: perhaps you don't have the time that others have to become a full time investor. Perhaps you don't have the inclination. Perhaps you want all the benefits with none of the drawbacks: you want the baby without the labour pains!

Perhaps you already love what you do and you just want to take the money and run? Perhaps you want to accelerate your earning time by not having to go through the experience process [because you want to earn on your portfolio in the meantime]? Perhaps you want to utilise [leverage] the knowledge and experience of the experts who are already doing it for themselves?

If this is the case then we can help you, and would love to help you.

We can save you time and make you money by building and managing a hands-free Property portfolio that you can retire on; enjoying financial independence.

You can read the testimonials at the front of the book or here, after all, evidence is important:

www.progressiveproperty.co.uk/testimonials.asp

We can help you if you are young or not so young. If you have savings or equity in your Property then we can build you a portfolio that at current rates will comfortably earn you well in excess of **£50,000** per year tax free [at just over 5% growth]. All you will have to do is sign papers. You can have an asset base that has cost you nothing in time but given you choice, freedom, passive income and something to pass on to your children [if you have/plan to have any].

Perhaps you want to do both. Perhaps you would like to earn while you are learning and you would like to learn from us. The point is you can and you have the choice now.

If you would like us to help you it couldn't be simpler. You can reach either or both of us at the following now:

Rob Moore & Mark Homer

Call us:

0845 1309505

Email us:

robmoore@progressiveproperty.co.uk

markhomer@progressiveproperty.co.uk

Enquire on our website:

www.progressiveproperty.co.uk

Reserve a seat at our next open day and see us speak:

www.progressiveproperty.co.uk/open-day-offer

Join in on a tele-seminar/webinar:

www.progressiveproperty.co.uk/squeeze/teleseminar/telesemin ar-signup.asp

Sign up for our free newsletter:

www.progressiveproperty.co.uk/newsletter-nomenu.asp

Buy a copy of "Make Cash in a Property Market Crash"

www.progressiveproperty.co.uk/book2-buy-now.asp

We would love to chat to you; or even better, meet you personally.

As you know, we love people who take action. Everything in this book is about becoming informed and them making a commitment to taking immediate and decisive action now to create the life that you want and deserve.

Procrastination is a disease and life rewards momentum.

Because of this, because of your commitment of money and time to go through this journey with us, we have a special, limited, once only offer for You now.

Let us warn you, this is **only** for you if you are **serious** about creating **long term wealth.**

You may also need to meet out criteria to become one of our close community of successful Property investors, and it is a mouth watering offer, that if you read the next section now, you may be able to take advantage of.

But only if you are serious now...

Rob Moore & Mark Homer

# Are You sitting on an Asset

Over 50 % of people *don't even know* that they can do this...

How would you like to be financially independent, living your life of choice, with no loss of your time, all from the equity you have in your house, right now?

And you don't even have to sell your house or pay anything out of your own pocket or earnings.

Imagine creating your dream life from an asset that you already have now...

It is simple, easy to follow, will take you very little time and you can start right away without any knowledge of Property.

So many people who have become financially independent have accessed their money through remortgage of their existing home. Many of them have gone on to become multi-millionaires. You can do the same now.

Many people didn't even realise the asset they were literally sitting on. Do you remember earlier in the book we asked you to think about your home: what you bought it for and what it is now worth? Or if you have a family member who has a house and you can ask them the same question...

Rob Moore & Mark Homer

The major benefit of this strategy is that your income and savings are not impacted in any way. If you have a Property with sufficient equity in it you could use the following strategy to invest without increasing your outgoings:

A typical example:

Your existing Property [home]:
Property worth £250,000
Repayment mortgage of £100,000 at £700pcm approx
£150,000 equity

Your re-mortgage:

New mortgage of £212,500 (85% of £250,000)
New interest only repayments of £1,325pcm approx
Old mortgage paid off leaving *£112,500* (less fees)

Investment Strategy:

Bank Contingency of £23,000
Invest £59,500
Bank increase in mortgage payments for 6 years: £30,000

With no change to your current circumstances you can set up your long term future for life now. Think about whether you want to use strategy 1, strategy 2 or both.

This is a typical example that someone would use when they

invest with us at Progressive. We help you turn one Property into 6 in 6 years, and help you earn 6 times as much per year without having to work at it.

Imagine now what that could mean for your life. Actually take a little time to picture it...

It has taken us over 5 years of buying Property to refine a system that can make Property investment accessible to most people. We have created a systemised 'Property Buying Machine,' that takes the human error out of successful Property investment

It is not for everyone; it is only for you if you are serious about creating long term wealth, but it can be for you if:

- You want it to be
- You have equity in your home that is sitting idle and not being leveraged. You have a redundancy, you have sold a business, have a divorce settlement or have access to cash
- You want to earn a passive income of over £50,000 per year, tax free without working or using your own time
- You want all of the benefits of Property investment, especially the cash, but do not want to spend years trying to become an expert

Rob Moore & Mark Homer

If you have a home that you own with a reasonable amount of equity in it, [90% of the people who are already doing it did it this way] then you should be very excited now.

Remember earlier in the book we talked about the relationship between money, work and stress? Maybe you don't want to continue working forever for 50 hours a week with little hope for future wealth and happiness in a job you don't like, with people you don't like. The government will *not* look after you and your family and your pension will probably not give you the lifestyle you want.

Maybe you imagine peace of mind and security; something that can help you enjoy the finer things in life, whatever they are to you. Perhaps even a little fun and adventure? If you don't want any of the stress but you want all of the benefits of more than enough money to retire with, then you can have it all, now.

So if you're serious about long term wealth you need to log on now to:

www.progressiveproperty.co.uk/save15k.asp

This offer of saving £15,000 will only last for a very limited time, for this particular [and small] run of this book. We like to produce small runs of the book so that we can keep updating it and improving it; and only get a few thousand printed at any one time, which usually sell very fast. It is open to 3 people at any one time and there are 1,000's of people who are reading this book right now:

www.progressiveproperty.co.uk/save15k.asp

For more information all you have to do is ask. Remember it is immediate action that gets results:

Call us:
0845 1309505

Email us:
robmoore@progressiveproperty.co.uk
markhomer@progressiveproperty.co.uk

Enquire on our website:
www.progressiveproperty.co.uk

Reserve a seat at our next open day:
www.progressiveproperty.co.uk/events.asp

Sign up for our free newsletter:
www.progressiveproperty.co.uk/newsletter-nomenu.asp

Join in on a tele-seminar/webinar:
www.progressiveproperty.co.uk/squeeze/teleseminar/teleseminar-signup.asp

Buy a copy of "Make Cash in a Property Market Crash"
www.progressiveproperty.co.uk/book2-buy-now.asp

Rob Moore & Mark Homer

# A final note [on a post it]

Well there is nothing left to say. Now you have to make your own choice. Are you going to take action on what you have read and be one of the few that succeed? Or are you going to change nothing, do nothing and still talk of when you were thinking about investing in Property all those years ago.

We find it quite strange that most people have access to the information that they need to go out there and take the life that they want, yet when faced with that seemingly simple choice, they still make the one they always made: the wrong one.

Of course that is not you. You are not like that. Just by reading this book you have proven that you want something more. Out of every thousand people who have been exposed to this book, only **you and one other** have made it this far. An amazing statistic isn't it?

And only one of the two of you left will go out and take action now. We sincerely hope it is you.

Please accept the biggest thank you for reading our book and being a significant part in a huge chapter in both of our lives; we look forward to speaking to you personally now.

Rob Moore & Mark Homer

# About Mark & Rob

This seems like a good time to tell you a little more about us.

This book is not about us, it is about what you can do with your financial future and how you can have security and wealth through Property. However you could be asking the question:

"Who are these guys and why should I trust them?"

Just before we start, we have decided, after saying we would never do it, and because of constant pressure, to run some mentorship programmes. It will only be Mark who is doing them. They will be strictly limited to one day per person and one person per week. Mark's time is currently worth over £500 per hour to our business and although he absolutely loves doing it, we can only afford for him to do a select few.

If you would feel that what you have read in this book is of value and you would like to be personally shown by Mark how to buy Property at 30% below market value over and over, then this might be for you. If you log on now and find that the offer has expired, you were just a little too late! If you hurry now you can save 78% by logging on to the special link below as a reader of this book

www.progressiveproperty.co.uk/mentorships.asp

Rob Moore & Mark Homer

OK. We absolutely regard ourselves as 2 normal guys. We are not 'Guru's' or self proclaimed cult leaders or evangelists. We don't have a long CV of master degrees and diplomas as there are no such qualifications in the Property 'industry.' Even if there were, they would probably mean very little to us, because we like to be able to give real life evidence and experience.

We both started from relatively humble beginnings and are by no means self professed Property squillionaires. We do have a relatively substantial Property portfolio that we have built in a relatively short space of time and we do have the evidence to back up our claims.

We have attended seminar after seminar [some good and some ridiculous] and have been on many courses. We have 7 years combined experience in Property [and we don't mean living in our Mum's house].

We have learned what works and what does not through actual experience. You will not find us on The Rich List [yet!] or talked about on Forbes, but we believe that we are humbly successful and do not need to shout too loudly outside of this book.

What is also so important is that we have a true passion for investing. Just the talk of investing money, finding deals with the potential to yield greater returns and building an asset base that can fund a fast and exciting lifestyle, turns us both on big time!

Sad, isn't it? Well actually, we don't think so. Some people like fast cars. Some people like fast women. Some people like both. Some people like shopping.

We love deals [and fast cars and women!]. We love the fun and the challenge [and sometimes the reward of beating the odds]. We built Progressive Property around this and the contentment and value in being able to help you do the same is also a huge driver for us.

We started Progressive Property on £300 each and we are proud of what we have been able to achieve for ourselves and our close community of investors, in a relatively short space of time.

## Mark about Mark

I had dreams of becoming an investment banker because it seemed like they earned the most money, had the most glamorous lifestyle and the most *fun*.

I soon realised that the competition was intense and I would not even be considered with my grades [although I enjoyed university very much]. I hit a wall because I had been working to this point for many years of my life.

I made money in the interim in true entrepreneurial fashion

selling various products; importing and exporting and such, and raised enough capital to be able to start investing.

Following University I went on to work for a multinational company on a graduate scheme. I thought I would be an integral part of a big company with great prospects.

As it turns out I was a glorified butcher earning average money with little future. I didn't like the corporate 'way' and the hierarchy. Looking up at someone's ass on a ladder I was at the bottom of was not my idea of happiness and freedom; having to wait in line for mediocre 'success' and 'status.'

I looked at the guys 20 years ahead of me and I didn't like what I saw. They were wrinkled, tired, financially stretched and they never looked happy. I thought to myself; all that work [weekends as well], and this is where I will be heading in 20 years?

Who wants to be like that?

Not me. No Thank You! I wasn't that happy. My zest, enjoyment and passion had been sapped.

I joined a Property investment company thinking that I could change my life by becoming a business owner. I was made a director for impressive Property sales however the reality was that I was a glorified employee. My boss certainly didn't look happy or live the kind of life which I aspired to, even though he 'read all of the books' and 'did not deal with negativity.' I didn't want to model him.

I was genuinely down at this point; nothing seemed to be going right. I wasn't sleeping for months on end because of the worry of work, and it began to affect my personal and working life.

Yeah on the outside I had the job title, yeah I was investing, and yes I was making money. But I wasn't happy.

And that is what is most important for me. For all of us, I think. Then I met Rob. He joined the company I was at and we hit it off immediately. He was [and still is] a qualified life coach.

We struck up a gentleman's deal that he would coach me in areas like relationships, health/body, work, spirituality and I would teach him how to invest and make money.

This is where my whole life changed. We got on so well and our skills seemed to dovetail. Whatever Rob was weak at I could help him with and vice versa.

Over a period of months I learned how to develop every area of my life to become the best that I could be. I started to run faster and longer than I had ever before (I now go almost everyday and for 2 months I ran every single day). I ran a half marathon after 4 months of training and have lost a lot of weight to become fit and healthy.

Even the girls started to notice me more [I think]! I became so much better at building relationships with people and I started to feel great and love every day of my life. Now I sleep like a baby and have massive energy all day long [as long as I have been for my run].

And you know the best bit?

My Property investment ability rocketed! We bought around 20 properties in 2006 with a relatively small amount of money and refined a Property buying system so much that we now get 15-30% discounts on *existing* (not new build) Property deals all day long.

I am now happier than I have ever been in my life. Don't get me wrong, I am not a happy clappy faux positive personal development junkie. I have my moments, but I know that I am in control of my feelings, my decisions, my actions and my future, which has been a huge development in my life, and something I never truly understood before.

I am lucky [Rob does not believe in luck but I think we have had our fair share] to be where I am and have the ability and knowledge to help you do the same.

# Rob about Mark

Mark is a dealmaker. He loves being on the phone and juggling many tasks at once. He has a sixth sense for Property investment deals in my opinion, and is definitely one of the most [if not *the* most] knowledgeable investors both here in Peterborough, and who I have met anywhere.

He bought some quite amazing deals in 2004/2005 when he was relatively new to the market and it was clear to me that I had to learn what he knew. He had a talent and was only going to get better. I wanted in on those kinds of deals.

He has helped me immensely with my Property knowledge and just being around him helps me grow immeasurably every single day.

His attention to detail is scary. To be honest sometimes he bores the pants off me with the amount of detail he goes into, but it's all good. I am one of these kinds of people who likes the baby and not the labour pains. I like to leverage and maximise my own time by positioning myself with people who are better than me in specialised areas. Mark actually enjoys the labour pains I think! That is one of the reasons why he is so good at what he does.

Rob Moore & Mark Homer

# Rob about Rob

Ever since I was 17 my life seemed to go steadily downhill.

I was a talented sportsman and blitzed A's at my GCSE's [through hard work and the fear of failure, rather than talent]. I was accepted to one of the best Universities in the country and felt I had a good future ahead of me [or so I thought]...

Then in 1996 I had 2 serious injuries within the space of 6 months. I crashed my motorbike [and not by half]. It was my pride and joy at the time because I no longer looked the pillock that I did on the moped I had previously. It took me one year of begging to let my parents get me one. I spent 6 months in rehabilitation from multiple breaks. [If you are considering getting a motorbike: DON'T! Just don't].

That ruined any prospect of me becoming a professional Golfer or Cricketer, which I had genuine aspirations for. I held much resentment and never really recovered from that. 6 months later my appendix burst [a close run in with the big man upstairs!] whilst in a nightclub. The whole second year of my A-Levels was written off.

I spent the next 7 years always living in the shadow of myself and what I could have become, but felt had been taken away from me. I lost my ability to dream and believe in myself, which sucked to be honest.

I managed to scrape into a University and pulled off a good degree in Architecture [fear of failure again]. As soon as I graduated all I wanted to do was anything else other than Architecture. The only reason I didn't quit the course after 2 months was my pride [ego] as I did not want anyone to think that I gave up on things.

Ironically this was to serve me very well for the future.

I came back to Peterborough to help my family in their pub as my Dad was very ill. What was essentially a 3 month plan ended up being nearly 3 years. All the while I knew that this was not what I ultimately wanted to do, but it is hard to break away when you think you are letting your family down. I'm sure you may have felt the same. I finally broke away in 2003 and set out to make a living in my real true passion: Art.

I have loved Art since before I could talk and that is something that I did actually have some kind of talent for. I believed that talent was enough to bring me the success, wealth and happiness that I desired.

As it turns out talent was not enough and I began to feel dragged down. I struggled for 2 years working 16 hours a day and failing to pay my debts of over £30,000 that I amassed at [and since] university. [If I had read the sales and marketing section of this book back then I think things would have been very different!].

Rob Moore & Mark Homer

I felt pretty low at this point. It was impacting other areas of my life such as my relationships with friends and family and my ability to socialise and enjoy life. I had completely lost my drive and enthusiasm. I was useless.

I was constantly looking back at what I should have been and that, 7 years on, I had still achieved nothing in my life that I wanted.

I realised that I had no savings, no future, and that if something happened to me I would be in big trouble. I was not looking forward to working 16 hours a day for the rest of my life. I mean, who wants that?

My dad worked for 15 years in the RAF serving his country to receive a pension of £19 per week. £19 per week. What an absolute joke. I did not want the same fate.

My Dad is nearly 63 and still working [sometimes 15 hours a day]. That has become a huge motivator for me to succeed financially so that I can help my family and ensure the same thing does not happen to me, my sister, my close friends, and people just like you.

I knew that I was missing something and in 2005 I met Mark, my business partner, great friend and investment partner. And co-author of this book, of course.

Those 2 months were the best, most exciting turning points in my life. Since then, since finding what I consider to be my purpose and true path, everything has accelerated so fast and I have learned so much that sometimes I wonder what on earth I was doing for 25 years.

Mark and I really have had the most amazing journey and I feel very fortunate [not lucky] to have forged such a relationship with such a great guy, and someone with such vast knowledge.

I was out of debt by April and in the same year [my interest payments alone were over £2,000 per month - more than I was earning!], I reached a £1 million Property portfolio [most of which was gained through one simple remortgage of my existing house], trained as a life coach, did a coaching TV show for Living TV and became MD of a Property investment company.

I really don't consider this to be 'impressive.' I have a healthy caution towards 'life coaching' and Property investment, because many people are not **diligent** enough to be able to do it properly. However we're all just trying to make a living and with the right amount of application both are seriously rewarding for very different reasons.

I feel that is an area where I have vastly improved over the last few years, because my biggest problem was getting quite good at things but not taking it that extra step. I learned that is was the experts; the best of the best, who make all of the money.

Rob Moore & Mark Homer

I honestly feel that the reason I have achieved more in the last 2 years than the previous 25 and a half is not because I am anything special, but because I am doing what I truly believe in and what I have a real passion for.

If only I had started sooner, but then I guess we all say that, don't we? And I now know that **Now** is always the best time.

It's funny because so many people think they have missed the boat with Property. I thought that myself for about 4 years. I was looking at 3 bed houses for £70,000 in 2003. And I did nothing [but watch them go up and up and up and tell people stories about why I didn't couldn't wouldn't shouldn't buy them!]. These are worth over £200,000 now. I am just so glad that I know what I know now. Now is always the best time.

Things just keep moving for Mark and I now and we have newer, bigger goals. We have finished writing our second book and building our portfolio both for us and our investors daily. We've had offers to do TV shoes, endless joint ventures and business partner alliances, and met some really great people. It is amazing what a bit of momentum can do. It is the security that I feel from having a Property portfolio that will look after me for the rest of my life that enables me to really go for it in other areas too.

# Mark about Rob

It's Rob's drive and focus that inspire me the most. When I first met him he knew only the basics about Property, but within his first 9 months his portfolio was up over £1million [and he was £30,000 in debt at the time].

I have not met many people who have the ability to do this and the fact that he has done it in a very short space of time gives me the evidence I need to know that you can do the same.

Rob encouraged me to start out on our own and we haven't looked back since. I think it is his ability to just go for it and make things work regardless of what people say that keeps us going when many people have been saying [through the last 5 years] that the Property market is dead. If we believed them we would still be employed and not have the freedom we desire; which is so important.

He learns very quickly and has seriously added to his skills since I have known him. Sometimes he thinks so much to the future that he forgets about detail, and I have had to help him with his driving licence, a couple of parking tickets, the odd speeding fine and some household insurance.

I'm not his Mum or his P.A, but we all have to make sacrifices I guess!

Rob Moore & Mark Homer

# Your figures & projections

Rob Moore & Mark Homer

## Your rules: Page 89

Enjoy filling in the questions below, they are tested and just writing them down will increase your chances 10 fold of achieving them. Remember; be as specific as You can:

**Your Vision, Big picture & Purpose:**
[Wealth to change the world? A higher standard of living for you and the ones you love? Shelter or charity? Freedom? Financial Independence? A collection of supercars?]

_____

_____

_____

_____

_____

_____

_____

_____

_____

_____

_____

_____

_____

_____

_____

_____

Rob Moore & Mark Homer

**Where are You Now? Your Equity statement:** page 94
[State exactly where you are. Subtract your total debt from the equity in your assets and your savings. It's great to go back to this year after year to see your progress]:

Equity in assets:

_____

_____

Cash & savings:

_____

_____

Fixed expenses [pcm or pa]:

_____

_____

Estimated variable expenses [pcm or pa]:

_____

_____

Value of Possessions:

_____

_____

All debt ex. mortgages [loans, credit cards, hp etc]

_____

_____

Total personal equity [equity in assets + cash – debt]:

_____

_____

## What specifically do You want to enable you to achieve Your goals?

[How many properties do you want in your portfolio. How much cash do you want per year? Is it passive? Do you want to work or retire, and by what date? Property full time, part time or leveraged? This is your means of getting your goals]:

_____

_____

_____

_____

_____

_____

_____

_____

_____

_____

_____

_____

_____

_____

_____

_____

_____

_____

_____

_____

_____

**Your goals:**

[Best selling author? Property expert status? A self built mansion? A collection of supercars? 10 properties? 100 properties? Body building world champion? Pro golfer? Lady of leisure married to James Bond? Go for it; everything that you want]

_____

_____

_____

_____

_____

_____

_____

_____

_____

_____

**Your unique talents, skills, expertise and qualities:** Page 130
[Don't be shy, we all have them. Anything at all, you might be surprised]

_____

_____

_____

_____

_____

_____

_____

and a few more lines, because there is always more!

_____

_____

_____

_____

_____

_____

_____

**Property buying rules example:** page 99
[Generic & always subject to improvement]

**Strategy:**
Buy and hold for long term. Looking for capital growth through natural market movements and forced appreciation through regeneration and increase in demand.

Property must be at worst net cash flow neutral against our Property Buying Spreadsheet.

**Property Type:**
Ex local authority, 1&2 bed flats with ground rents/maintenance less than £500 per year. 2 & 3 bed houses, not new build; 5 years old or more; preferably 1970's period conversions in city centres. No structural defects. Nothing above shops, restaurants etc.

**Property Location:**
Peterborough only until supply runs low, within 15 miles of city centre office: in specific areas already defined by yield of 6% or better. Must be lettable within 1 week and demand should already be identified.

**Valuation:**
Look for streets where values are established and comparables exist as a means of correctly identifying end values and relative discounts.

**Yield:**
Gross yield 6% or better. Property must not shortfall after all costs or produce a cash out that covers the shortfall for 5 years or more. Compare against actual net yield figures through previous data.

**Property Value:**
Between £50,000 and £120,000 with specific focus on £65,000 to £95,000 purchase price.

# The Law of compounding: Page 69

On Page 69 we were discussing the figures using the Rule of 72 and the Laws of compounding and leverage.

Here are the calculations behind the figures shown on Page 68/9

The Rule of 72:
5% growth: 72/5 = 14.4 years to turn £5,000 into £10,000
8% growth: 72/8 = 9 years to turn £5,000 into £10,000
11.74% growth: 72/11.74 = 6 years 48 days to turn £5,000 into £10,000

Property growth on the example £100,000 Property in 10 years:
5% growth: £100,000 becomes £162,889
8% growth: £100,000 becomes £215,892
11.74% growth: £100,000 becomes £303,450

Example capital employed [spent] to purchase a Property worth £100,000 for £85,000: £5,000

[This example takes into account all fees of buying a Property such as valuations, conveyancing, solicitors fees and legal work, Land registry and transfer fees, office copy and disbursements, broker fees and so on. Using our suggested investment model, you would get your £15,000 deposit back, therefore it is not employed or spent capital].

Rob Moore & Mark Homer

Therefore, using the example of 11.74% growth every year for 10 years, your growth would be:

Total Property value: £303,450

minus existing mortgage: £85,000 = £218,450

£218,450/5000 = 4369% return on your capital spent [ROCE]

# Cost of capital: Page 102

*Option 1:* You invest the £20,000 and with it, using your increasing knowledge, you can plausibly buy 1 property per year with the same capital. For ease of figures; these properties are worth £100,000 based on today's figures.

Compounded equity at end of yr 5 [based on 5% growth]: £168,461

Property 1: Value after year 5: £127,628
Property 2: Value after year 5: £127,628
Property 3: Value after year 5: £127,628
Property 4: Value after year 5: £127,628
Property 5: Value after year 5: £127,628

Total value: £638,140

Less 5 mortgages of £469,679

£638,140 - £469,679 = **£168,461**

# Interest only vs. repayment: Page 106

On Page 106 we were discussing the benefits of interest only mortgages. Here is a full breakdown of the figures.

It is assumed that the strategies in this book have been followed and the initial value of the properties purchased was £115,000. All of the properties bought in the next 15 years are all of the same relative type, and all increase at 8% per year.

It is also assumed that the properties are bought in blocks of 5 in 5 year increments. You can also buy at 1 per year and this would compound the figures even more. We really are trying to keep it simple, so stick with us.

For example: in the first year properties would be bought at £115,000. In the sixth year properties would be bought at £182,491 [£115,000 plus 6 years growth at 8% per year].

Year 5: 5 properties bought at £168,973 = £844,864
Year 10: 5 properties bought at £248,277 = £1,241,384
Year 15: 5 properties bought at £364,800 = £1,824,000

After 25 years the whole portfolio has gone up as follows:
Year 5 portfolio: 5 x £787,574 = £3,937,873
Year 10 portfolio: 5 x £787,574 = £3,937,873
Year 15 portfolio: 5 x £787,574 = £3,937,873
Total portfolio = **£11,813,649**

Rob Moore & Mark Homer

# The Art of finance & borrowing money:
## Page 239

Your house on your old mortgage: £250,000 going up at 10% per year: £25,000 [compounding] per year.

Compounded growth on £250,000 for 10 years at 10% per year:

Year 1: value: £250.000:        growth: £25,000
Year 2: value £275,000:        growth: £27,500
Year 3: value: £302,500:        growth: £30,250
Year 4: value £332,750:        growth: £33,275
Year 5: value £366,025:        growth: £36,602
Year 6: value £402,627:        growth: £40,263
Year 7: value £442,890:        growth: £44,289
Year 8: value £487,179:        growth: £48,718
Year 9: value £535,897:        growth: £53,590
Year 10: value £589,487:        growth: £58,949

Your new portfolio:
6 properties [your house plus 5 investments]: £1,000,000 [conservative estimate of your Property plus 5 properties in 6 years] going up at 10% per year: £100,000 [compounding] per year.

Compounded growth on £1,000,000 for 10 years at 10% per year:

Year 1: value: £1,000,000:     growth: £100,000
Year 2: value £1,100,000:      growth: £110,000
Year 3: value: £1,210,000:     growth: £121,000
Year 4: value £1,331,000:      growth: £133,100
Year 5: value £1,464,100:      growth: £146,410
Year 6: value £1,610,510:      growth: £156,051
Year 7: value £1,771,561:      growth: £177,156
Year 8: value £1,948,717:      growth: £194,872
Year 9: value £2,143,589:      growth: £214,359
Year 10: value £2,357,948:     growth: £235,795

# Capital gains & IHT: Page 323

*Progressive thinking*: own 11 properties using equity from your first home. Total portfolio value in 2025: **£4million** [conservative estimate of only 5% growth].

**This is how you do it:**

You own one Property worth £250,000 in 2007. You release equity of £150,000. You use £115,000 to buy 10 properties and have a contingency of £35,000.

It takes you 10 years to buy 10 properties [one per year] which grow at **5%** per year. The results after 25 years are as follows:

Your Property value: £250,000         Value at year 25: £846,589
Investment Property 1: £125,000       Value at year 25: £423,294
Investment Property 2: £131,250       Value at year 25: £423,294
Investment Property 3: £137,813       Value at year 25: £423,294
Investment Property 4: £144,703       Value at year 25: £423,294
Investment Property 5: £151,938       Value at year 25: £423,294
Investment Property 6: £159,535       Value at year 25: £423,294
Investment Property 7: £167,512       Value at year 25: £423,294
Investment Property 8: £175,888       Value at year 25: £423,294
Investment Property 9: £184,682       Value at year 25: £423,294
Investment Property 10: £193,916      Value at year 25: £423,294

Total portfolio value from equity in one Property: **£5,079,533**

Rob Moore & Mark Homer

These are the same figures at 8% growth:

Your Property value: £250,000   Value at year 25: £1,712,119
Investment Property 1: £125,000   Value at year 25: £856,059
Investment Property 2: £135,000   Value at year 25: £856,059
Investment Property 3: £145,800   Value at year 25: £856,059
Investment Property 4: £157,464   Value at year 25: £856,059
Investment Property 5: £170,061   Value at year 25: £856,059
Investment Property 6: £183,666   Value at year 25: £856,059
Investment Property 7: £198,359   Value at year 25: £856,059
Investment Property 8: £214,228   Value at year 25: £856,059
Investment Property 9: £224,939   Value at year 25: £856,059
Investment Property 10: £242,935 Value at year 25: £856,059

Total portfolio value from equity in one Property: **£10,272,713**

# 5 The magic number: Page 333

5 Property portfolio growth at 8% per year:

Property 1 in 1st year:
value £125,000.   Value in year 5: £170,061
Property 2 in 2nd year:
value £135,000.   Value in year 5: £170,061
Property 3 in 3rd year:
value £145,800.   Value in year 5: £170,061
Property 4 in 4th year:
value £157,464.   Value in year 5: £170,061
Property 5 in 5th year:
value £170,061.   Value in year 5: £170,061

Total value: **£850,306**

5 Property portfolio growth at 5% per year:

Property 1 in 1st year:
value £125,000.   Value in year 5: £151,938
Property 2 in 2nd year:
value £131,250.   Value in year 5: £151,938
Property 3 in 3rd year:
value £137,813.   Value in year 5: £151,938
Property 4 in 4th year:
value £144,703.   Value in year 5: £151,938
Property 5 in 5th year:
value £151,938.   Value in year 5: £151,938
Total value: **£759,691**

5 Property portfolio at historical growth of 11.74% per year:

Property 1 in 1st year:
value £125,000.   Value in year 5: £194,869
Property 2 in 2nd year:
value £139,675.   Value in year 5: £194,869
Property 3 in 3rd year:
value £156,073.   Value in year 5: £194,869
Property 4 in 4th year:
value £174,396.   Value in year 5: £194,869
Property 5 in 5th year:
value £194,869.   Value in year 5: £194,869

Total value: **£974,349**

Equity in your portfolio at 8% growth:

[Total value of Property minus initial 85% mortgage]:

Property 1 in 1st year: value £170,061.   Equity: £63,811
Property 2 in 2nd year: value £170,061.   Equity: £55,311
Property 3 in 3rd year: value £170,061.   Equity: £46,131
Property 4 in 4th year: value £170,061.   Equity: £36,217
Property 5 in 5th year: value £170,061.   Equity: £25,509

Total equity: **£226,979**

To reserve a copy of our latest book "Make Cash in a Property Market Crash" whilst they last [very relevant right now and we may pull them when the market changes] please visit:

www.progressiveproperty.co.uk/book2-buy-now.asp

Rob Moore & Mark Homer

Remember that You can be, do and have anything you want. Never let the others and the voices tell you otherwise. Take care now...

Rob Moore & Mark Homer